# Orr's Truisms

## 2

### Bert K. Orr

Orr's Truisms 2© 2009, Bert K. Orr. All rights reserved.

No part of this book may be used or reproduced in any form or by any means, or stored in a database or retrieval system without the prior written permission of the publisher, except in the case of brief quotations embodied in critical articles or reviews. Making copies of any part of this book for any purpose other than your own personal use is a violation of United States copyright laws. Entering any of the contents into a computer for mailing list or database purposes is strictly prohibited unless written authorization is obtained from the owner.

ISBN 1441446370
EAN 9781441446374

Cover and interior design by TFS

# Forward

*A 'Truism' is a statement, the truth of which is obvious or well known.*

I don't know when I started collecting 'truisms' or exactly why. I have always been fascinated by inspirational thoughts and a voracious reader, so I guess it just happened.

As I wrote them down and the collection started to grow, I then needed to do something with all of these random thoughts.

Several years ago I started finding willing volunteers to type up five or six sheets at a time, then I would start giving them out to friends or people that I encountered who were soon to become friends. This grew into a list of eighty-plus 'friends' all over the country and who are on my quarterly mailing list.

Some just enjoy the smiles, some can't wait for new material for speeches and newsletters, but for me it's a way to stay connected with people I have encountered over my ninety years here on planet earth. After I do a mailing, I get phone calls and notes from all over the country. In these days of hurry and rush it's a wonderful thing.

I hope you enjoy this second book as much as the first.

*Bert K. Orr*

*Acknowledgment:*

A heart filled "thank you" to Chuck and Tom Shubnell – brothers and good friends who suggested and compiled these books. Also, thanks to all that went before, there is 'no such thing as an original thought' and this second book is another collection of a multitude of funny, wonderful, and inspirational thoughts that I have collected over many decades, whose authors go unnamed.

*We should all live as though someone were writing a book about us.*

# Table of Contents

Time and Ageing ................................................................... 7

Friendship and Kindness ..................................................... 27

Happiness and Humor ......................................................... 47

Health and Fitness ............................................................... 57

Adversity .............................................................................. 69

Success and Failure ............................................................. 73

Life ....................................................................................... 93

Bert's Observations ........................................................... 107

Love ................................................................................... 139

Leadership ......................................................................... 147

Family and Home .............................................................. 151

Orr's Laws ......................................................................... 171

Children ............................................................................. 179

Knowledge and Wisdom ................................................... 189

Politics and Law ................................................................ 203

Wealth ................................................................................ 211

All Creatures Great and Small .......................................... 225

Dictionary .......................................................................... 231
    Index .............................................................................. 239
    Endnote ......................................................................... 245

# Time and Ageing

## Time and Ageing

The best time to do something worthwhile is between yesterday and tomorrow.

Promise yourself more moments like this.

The way each day will look to you all starts with who you're looking to.

Today is the first day of your life, but relax! So is tomorrow!

Why worry about tomorrow? Who knows what will hit you today?

Let not the mistakes of yesterday or the fears of tomorrow spoil today.

We must strive to die young at a very old age.

Winter is the time when you try to keep your home as warm as it was in summer when you complained about it.

Youth has no age.

Don't worry about losing hair; think of it as gaining face.

Age is something that doesn't matter, unless you are a cheese.

Ever notice how we get older so much faster than we grow up?

I like time clocks. After a really bad day, it's nice to have something to punch.

Whatever makes me tick needs winding.

Memories are keepsakes of the happy times we've known.

Cherish all your happy moments; they make a fine cushion for old age.

A good snapshot stops a moment from running away.

The future belongs to those who create it.

Maturity is a high price to pay for growing up.

The first big shock of retirement is when you realize there are no days off.

# Time and Ageing

April hath put a spirit of youth in everything.

Time is a circus, always packing up and moving away.

Delay is the deadliest form of denial.

When you're young, you watch people. When you're mature, you watch out for people.

Class reunion: A gathering where you come to the conclusion that most of the people your own age are a lot older than you are.

About the only thing that comes without effort is old age.

The secret of staying young is to live honestly, eat slowly, and lie about your age.

To be quite oneself, one must first waste a little time.

They talk of the dignity of work. The dignity is in leisure.

Prediction is very difficult especially about the future.

Spring is nature's way of saying let's party!

Do not resent growing old, many are denied the privilege.

Truth has no special time of its own. Its hour is now - always.

Age does not diminish the extreme disappointment of having a scoop of ice cream fall from the cone.

Nothing makes a person more productive than the lost minute.

Yesterday is history. Tomorrow is a mystery and today is a gift; that's why they call it the present.

Everything takes longer than you expect.

It's not that age brings childhood back again; age merely shows what children we remain.

The time is always right to do what is right.

In the end it's not the years in your life that count. It's the life in your years.

Time and Ageing

The great thing about getting older is that you don't lose all the other ages you've been.

Spend the afternoon. You can't take it with you.

I stopped whining about not having enough time when I realized that we all have 24 hours a day.

Until you value yourself, you won't value your time. Until you value your time, you will not do anything with it.

It is never too late to be <u>what</u> you might have been.

It is never too late to be <u>who</u> you might have been.

A man who dares to waste an hour of time has not discovered the value of life.

Forty is the old age of youth, fifty is the youth of old age.

God put me on earth to accomplish a certain number of things, right now I'm so far behind I'll never die.

Our life is made entirely of moments multiplied.

Time and tide wait for no man.

Youth is when we are always hunting greener pastures, and middle age is when we can barely mow the one we've got.

Strike while the iron is hot.

We often get in quicker by the back door that by the front.

Start doing today what you wish to do well tomorrow.

A minute is a little thing, but minutes make the day.
So crowd in some kind deeds before it slips away.

If you wait, there will come nectarlike fair weather.

The days are too short and the nights aren't long enough.

Retirees know it all and have plenty of time to tell you about it.

Timely good deeds are nicer than afterthoughts.

## Time and Ageing

Daylight Savings Time is like cutting off one end of a blanket and sewing it on the other end.

There should be a better reward for promptness than having to wait for everyone else.

There won't be time to dwell in the past if we keep busy today.

Don't let the urgent crowd out the important.

Nostalgia is the sandpaper that removes the rough edges from the good old days.

At my age, I've got an achey, breaky everything.

Formula for youth: Keep your enthusiasm and forget your birthdays.

"Over the hill" means the hardest climb is over and the view is terrific.

Worried about tomorrow? You did that yesterday about today.

Setting a good example for the children takes all of the fun out of middle age.

Spring is the time when youth dreams and old age remembers.

Worry doesn't empty tomorrow of its problems; it simply empties today of its strength.

You know you are getting old when you know your way around, but don't feel like going.

The older the violin, the sweeter the music.

"In the nick of time" is an expression invented by a man who overslept one morning and had to shave in a hurry.

Being "over the hill" isn't so bad if the descent isn't too rapid.

Blessed is the person who is too busy to worry in the daytime and too sleepy to worry at night.

The best thing about spring is that it comes when it is most needed.

At the beginning of the year, we have another chance to carve a beautiful shape in our own landscape.

Time and Ageing

Worry is today's mouse eating tomorrow's cheese.

It's not how many hours you put in, but what you put into the hours that count.

Worry pulls tomorrow's cloud over today's sunshine.

Don't trouble trouble, till it troubles you.

You're only cooking up trouble when you stew about tomorrow.

We all need time alone: to think, to dream, to wonder.

Sleep on what you plan to do. Don't stay awake over what you have done.

There won't be time to dwell in the past if we keep busy today.

At the rate changes are occurring everywhere, anyone nostalgic for the "good old days" is yearning for last week.

The time to relax is when we don't have the time.

Middle age is that transition period between "pinch an inch" and "grab some flab".

The man of the hour is the person who rarely watches the clock.

I'm not afraid of tomorrow, for I have seen yesterday and I love today.

No day is over if it makes a memory.

Don't you just love those winter mornings when you don't have to get up at the crack of dawn to see the sunrise?

Moments are like little pockets of time crammed with all of life's possibilities.

Today turns a new page in the history of your life.

Good grooming and smart clothing may take years off a person's age, but you can't fool a flight of stairs.

The best eraser in the world is a good night's sleep.

The really frightening thing about middle age is the knowledge you'll grow out of it.

# Time and Ageing

The worst of all thieves is the one who steals your time.

Middle age is when you finally get your head together just in time to watch your body fall apart.

What we keep in memory is ours, unchanged forever.

Any person who took yesterday and planned for tomorrow is enjoying it today.

Time can wash away personal dirt, but stains must wear off.

Do you realize that tomorrow people will refer to today as 'the good old days'?

Most people 65 and older memorize their social security numbers. Those 35 to 65 know their credit card numbers by heart. Those 15 and under know cable channels.

The older a person gets, the farther he had to walk to school as a child.

People do not stop doing things because they get older. They get older because they stop doing things.

I don't mind being a procrastinator. In fact, I should have started sooner.

There is no sadder sight than immaturity grown to an old age.

Always put off until tomorrow what you shouldn't do at all.

You get a strong hint that it's middle-age when you feel every morning the way you used to feel, when you were coming down with something.

We are getting old when we are doing more and more things for the last time, and fewer and fewer things for the first time.

I wouldn't mind the rat race so much if there was more cheese to go around.

You never realize how short a month is until you start to pay alimony.

We should resolve to be more understanding of the very young, old, weak, and sick. Sometime in life you will have been all of them.

Inside every 70-year old is a teenager asking, "What happened?"

# Time and Ageing

If you can't become mean, nasty, and grumpy, what's the point of growing old?

A man does not become mature. He just gives up habits.

Why is it that a person your own age always looks older than you do?

The moment may be temporary, but the memory is forever.

One thing worse than forgetfulness is remembering things that never happened.

At the end of your days, be leaning forward, not falling backward.

You are older when what was called adventure is now called stress.

You're getting old when you're ready, willing, and able, but not at the same time.

Home is where you hang your memories.

He is about a year from retirement, but his brain retired about ten years ago.

God put me on earth to accomplish a certain number of things. Right now I'm so far behind, I will never die.

He who is deaf, dumb, and blind will live a hundred years in peace.

Why can't life's problems hit us when we are 18 and know all the answers?

Some days are a total waste of makeup.

If it wasn't for Monday mornings, Friday nights just wouldn't be the same.

Night falls but never breaks and day breaks and never falls.

Opportunity is not a lengthy visitor.

Maturity begins when we're content to feel we are right about something without feeling the necessity to prove someone else is wrong.

Retirement has nothing to do with doing nothing.

What is catastrophic for the young is mildly troubling to the old.

May each new day inspire you with peace and hope.

Memory is the diary we carry with us.

You can clutch the past so tightly that it leaves your arms too full to embrace the present.

Recall it as often as you wish. . . a happy memory never wears out.

Do your best today; tomorrow will be easier.

We are part of the same story, as long as one of us is still around to remember.

Past experience should be a guidepost, not a hitching post.

A true test of patience is not minding being put on hold.

Most people spend a lot of time dreaming about the future, never realizing a little arrives each day.

You can't turn back the clock. But you can wind it up again.

When an old person dies, a library is lost.

Today might not be so good, but tomorrow you get another chance to get it right.

You never know when you're making a memory.

I always wanted to be the last man on earth just to see if all those women were lying to me.

It's the fight itself that keeps you young.

It is better to look ahead and prepare than to look back and regret.

Age is a very high price to pay for maturity.

When your friends begin to flatter you on how young you look, it's a sure sign you're getting old.

An early morning walk is a blessing for the whole day.

Dream as if you'll live forever - live as if you'll die today.

## Time and Ageing

If you thought you were going to die tomorrow you'd know how to live today.

You will always find time for that which you place first.

The best thing about the future is that it only comes one day at a time.

Every man is the architect of his own future.

Forget the troubles that passed away, but remember the blessings that come each day.

Today is the day to make memories.

We cannot lose our faith in the future without first losing our memory of the past.

Don't let yesterday use up too much of today.

Anger is the only thing to put off till tomorrow.

Even if I knew the world was going to end tomorrow, I would plant a tree today.

We can improve our tomorrows with a better understanding of our yesterdays.

To better the future, know the past.

Sleep is like air - it doesn't seem all that important until you're not getting any.

We live our lives forward, but understand them backward.

Time is the wages of life; invest it, don't spend it.

Take a lesson from the clock - it passes time by keeping its hands busy.

This only is denied the gods: the power to remake the past.

As soon as people are old enough to know better, they don't know anything at all.

If you pull out a gray hair, seven will come to its funeral.

Instead of counting the days, make the days count.

# Time and Ageing

If you hem in both ends of your day with prayer, it won't be so likely to unravel in the middle.

Don't put off enjoyment - there's no time like the present.

With every rising of the sun, think of your life as just begun.

You can always recall moving an item to a safer place, but never recall where that place is.

God made time, but man made haste.

You are not old until it takes you longer to rest than it does to get tired.

I know not what the future holds, but I know who holds the future.

Time tells on a person, especially a good time.

Experience is a great advantage; the problem is that when you get the experience you're too damned old to do anything about it.

Millions long for immortality who don't know what to do with themselves on a rainy Sunday afternoon.

The average human heart beats 100,000 times a day. Make those beats count.

The trees that are slow to grow bear the best fruit.

The bitterest tears shed over graves are for words left unsaid and deeds left undone.

You cannot live a perfect day without doing something for someone who will never be able to repay you.

No day is so bad it can't be fixed with a nap.

One never knows what each day is going to bring. The important thing is to be open and ready for it.

Middle age is the awkward period when father time starts catching up with Mother Nature.

Autumn is a second Spring when every leaf is a flower.

There is no such thing in anyone's life as an unimportant day.

Time and Ageing

The trouble with making mental notes is that the ink fades so fast.

A person's age can be measured by the degree of pain one feels as one comes in contact with a new idea.

There are seven ways to warm your feet in February. Dipping them in the Caribbean is one. If you can afford that, forget the other six.

Do it tomorrow – you have made enough mistakes today.

August is that time of year when you go to turn on the air conditioner and it already is.

Most problems should be solved in the time spent worrying about them.

Time is not measured by years that we live,
but by the deeds that we do and the joys that we give.

This is the final test of a gentleman: His respect for those who can be of no possible value to him.

May your life be like a snowflake - leave a mark, but not a stain.

Today's tendency is tomorrow's custom.

One of the secrets of a long and fruitful life is to forgive everybody everything, every night before you go to bed.

The best preparation for tomorrow is to give life your best today.

You know you're getting old when you go duck hunting just to please the dog.

If you have something to say, to do, or to write, do it today, for in life there is not always a second chance.

The longer you keep your temper the more it will improve.

Spring - when Mother Nature begins to liquidate her frozen assets.

As people grow older, one of the things that makes them happy about putting on old clothes is the fact that they can.

When April rains come; some people see only puddles, while others see flowers.

## Time and Ageing

Nothing is as dangerous as being too modern. One is apt to grow old-fashioned quite suddenly.

People who wouldn't think of wasting money, squander time away each day.

Save the good times in your memory bank. There will come a day when you'll want to start making withdrawals.

As people grow older, they discover that most of the things they worry about never happen.

Old age begins the moment you trade in your dreams for memories.

Raising the retirement age is like moving the finish line when the horses are coming down the homestretch.

Nothing beats uncertainty, to make tomorrow more interesting.

Time is something that goes by slowly between paydays.

Don't worry about avoiding temptation. As you grow older, it will avoid you.

An old timer is some one who remembers when safe sex meant your parents had gone away for the weekend.

Tomorrow does not belong to you. Do it today.

Did you ever get the feeling that perhaps your gray hair isn't premature?

The measure of life is not its duration but its donation.

Youth is when life is filled with thrills.
Old age is when you are filled with pills.

Be life long or short, its completeness depends on what it was lived for.

None are as old as those who have outlived enthusiasm.

Many of us feel that we would like to return to the good old days; of course, we'd want to take television, air-conditioning, and our higher wages with us.

Regrets are the natural property of gray hairs.

Whatever old way you don't want to change was once the new way.

# Time and Ageing

At my age, it's always something I have to live with or something I have to live without.

To truly appreciate the dignity and beauty in an old face, you have to read between the lines.

Whatever poet, orator or sage may say of it, old age is still old age.

Every young man should know well at least one old man to whom he can go when he wants the teachings of experience rather than mere sympathy.

An old gentleman in a nursing home was reading his Bible.
A visitor came along and asked him what he was doing.
"Cramming for my final," he replied.

A man who's so today has timed his life all wrong. He was a child when everything was considered a child's fault, and he's a parent when everything is considered the parent's fault.

Don't count your years as they mount.
Instead do everything to make them count.

You can often tell what makes a person tick by how he unwinds.

Most people say: When you get old, you have to give things up. I say you get old because you give things up.

Age is kind only to those who do not hate it.

It takes most of an hour to look one's best.
It takes most of a lifetime to be one's best.

It is only the modern that ever becomes old-fashioned.

It's a shame that so many of the activities which make life enjoyable also make it shorter.

Spring is the time the youth dreams and old age remembers.

You know you're getting old when the candles cost more than the cake.

You know you are getting old when you know your way around, but don't feel like going.

Anyone observant enough to guess your age will annoy you in other ways, too.

## Time and Ageing

Men over seventy offer one the devotion of a lifetime.

One's past is what one is. It is the only way by which people should be judged.

Summer is the time we try to keep the house as cold as it was in the winter when we complained about it.

To get back one's youth one has merely to repeat one's follies.

The future has a way of arriving unannounced.

The only difference between the saint and the sinner is that every saint has a past, and every sinner has a future.

The trouble with class reunions is that old flames have become even older.

Tomorrow is often the busiest day of the week.

In old age you spend half of your time looking for a bathroom, and the other half trying to remember people's names.

After you retire, you spend half your time looking for things you lose.

Wrinkled was not one of the things I wanted to be when I grew up.

If you don't think every day is a good day, just try missing one.

The amount of sleep required by the average person is about ten minutes more.

Don't feel bad about growing old. Some people never get the chance.

You are young only once, but you can stay immature for life.

Children are the only people wise enough to enjoy today, without regretting yesterday or fearing tomorrow.

You are young and useful at any age if you are still planning for tomorrow.

How old are you madam?
I'm approaching forty
from which direction.

Age is a matter of the mind; if you don't mind, it doesn't matter.

Time is what keeps everything from happening at once.

Time and Ageing

Young at heart; slightly older in other places.

It's not the pace of life that concerns me, it's the sudden stop at the end.

She looked like she had been picked up by the heels and dipped in age.

I'm a man easy in my skin.

The only thing that comes without effort is old age.

The first hour of waking is the rudder that guides the whole day.

Time is a dressmaker specializing in alterations.

To be seventy years young is sometimes far more cheerful and hopeful than to be forty years old.

Waste of time is the most extravagant and costly of all expenses.

Time spent with friends and family is time worth remembering.

Age is just a number and mine is unlisted.

The trick is to live a long time without growing old.

At my age I can't see the forest or the trees.

Plan to be spontaneous, tomorrow.

If you want pleasant memories, you need to arrange for them in advance.

There is one thing about the new technology I like - it grows old faster than I do.

Time is a river without banks.

Lost wealth may be replaced by industry, lost knowledge by study, lost health by temperance or medicine, but lost time is gone forever.

The thing about being dead is that there's no future in it.

Despair is a foolish squandering of precious time.

There's definitely an energy crisis. It's called Monday morning.

Some weeks you really need Saturday on a Wednesday.

# Time and Ageing

Time flies - Spend it with people who mean the most to you.

One thing about growing older is that just when you reach the age when you start to get your head together, your body starts to fall apart.

I never think of the future. It comes soon enough.

Everything else you grow out of, but you never recover from childhood.

It is better to wear out than to rust out

To look back all the time is boring, excitement lies in tomorrow.

A grouch is a person who somehow can manage to find something wrong with even the good old days.

One can't help getting older, but one doesn't have to be old.

Eat one live toad in the morning, and nothing worse will happen to you the rest of the day.

If it wasn't for the last minute, nothing would get done.

Middle age is when your age starts to show around your middle.

One of the annoying disadvantages of maturity is now you really are old enough to know better.

I'm not afraid to die. I just don't want to be there when it happens.

The secret of staying young is to live honestly, eat slowly, and lie about your age.

If things get better with age then I'm magnificent.

All the gardens of yesterdays are in the roots of the past. All the flowers of our tomorrows are in the seeds of today.

At my age, getting lucky is finding my car in the parking lot.

Your thinking is OK until you start hiding your own Easter eggs.

Grow up as soon as you can, it pays. The only time you really live fully is from 30 to 60.

To men over 40: Don't worry about losing hair; think of it as gaining face.

Time and Ageing

Worry is wasting today's time cluttering up tomorrow's opportunities with yesterday's troubles.

History swings from left to right through time; it never walks a straight line.

We do not count a man's years, until he has nothing else to count.

Gratitude is the memory of the heart.

Longevity can be Hell, knowing things will inevitably go bad, but not knowing when.

When you are forty, half of you belongs to the past, and when you are seventy, nearly all of you does.

The glory of the past is an illusion. So is the glory of the present.

Nostalgia is like a grammar lesson - you find the present tense and the past perfect.

Time and wilted salad wait for no man.

If you wait until retirement to really start living, you've waited too long.

Nostalgia never gets old.

Regrets over yesterday and the fear of tomorrow are twin thieves that rob us of the moment.

Old men dream dreams - young men see visions.

There's no time like the present.

Some people spend the first half of their lives indulging in excesses that shorten the last half.

How we spend our days is, or course, how we spend our lives.

May you look back on the past with as much pleasure as you look forward to the future.

What we are when we are old is what we learned when we were young.

Prayer should be the key to the day and the lock of the night.

# Time and Ageing

Birthdays are such happy times. It's too bad they come on the same day you get another day older.

"Merry" is a word for Christmas.
"Happy" is a word for New Year's.
"Thanks" is a word for all year long.

Though no one can go back and make a brand new start, anyone can start from now and make a brand new end.

One of your greatest possessions is the 24 hours directly ahead of you.

Don't worry too much about today, in a couple of days, it will be yesterday and there is no sense in worrying about the past.

If you believe that the past can't be changed, you haven't read a celebrity's autobiography.

Our days are like identical suitcases, all the same size, but some people can pack more into them than others.

I wish I could stand on a busy corner, hat in hand, and beg people to throw me all their wasted hours.

A minute of action is better than an hour of worry.

Some people are slow to change their minds. Ask their age and they will give the same answer for years.

Real generosity towards the future lies in giving all to the present.

The one duty we owe to history is to rewrite it.

What the future has in store for you depends on what you have stored for the future.

When you depart, leave a vacuum, not a wake.

Time is the most valuable thing a man can spend.

The end isn't always where it should be.

Time and Ageing

# Friendship and Kindness

## **Friendship and Kindness**

If you were another person, would you like to have yourself as a friend?

You cannot possess one richer treasure than the loyalty of a friend.

Good friends are good for your health.

You can discover more about a person in an hour of play than in a year of conversation.

Three things in life are important. The first is to be kind. The second is to be kind. The third is to be kind.

One good thing about being wrong is the joy it brings to others.

Trouble is usually produced by those who produce nothing else.

If we live up to the best that is within us, we will easily discover the best in others.

No man is poor who has friends.

The most difficult things for a person to do are keep a secret, forget an injury, and make good use of leisure.

A bore is someone who talks when you want him to listen.

The worst trouble about peddling a half truth is that we may let out the wrong half.

A true test of a person's honesty is how quickly they will admit an error.

Ever notice when someone says you always have to have the last word, it's not you who has it?

All I have to do is keep him talking and I can watch his nose grow.

The one thing that unites all human beings regardless of age, gender, religion, economic status or ethnic background, is that, deep down inside, we all believe that we are above average drivers.

The most destructive force in the universe is gossip.

## Friendship and Kindness

You cannot do a kindness too soon, because you never know how soon it will be too late.

The weak can never forgive. Forgiveness is the attribute of the strong.

People with patience put up with people they would rather put down.

One joy scatters a hundred grieves.

Those who do as they please, seldom please anyone.

When you cannot get a compliment in any other way, pay yourself one.

Subtlety is the art of saying what you think and getting out of range before it is understood.

Some acts of kindness may not receive a lot of attention, but they are never forgotten.

A warm smile thaws an icy stare.

The song from beginning to end, I found in the heart of a friend.

Trust thyself only, and another shall not betray thee.

Warning: People who have an attitude know how to use it.

Plant kindness, harvest love.

Giving does not drain our resources, but provides a space for us to refill.

Our world has seen many different advances in communications, with satellites and other technology, but the quickest is still the wink.

Stay in touch; absence makes the heart go wander.

People are lonely because they build walls instead of bridges.

Kindness is the oil that takes the friction out of life.

The milk of human kindness should not be bottled up.

When a person is down, an ounce of help is better than a pound of preaching.

Busy people don't have time to be busybodies.

## Friendship and Kindness

Never put off until tomorrow a kindness you can do today.

Bless the parrot - it repeats what it hears without trying to 'spice it up'.

Every man is the architect of his own fortunes, but the neighbors superintend the construction.

Some people get up and go to the window and shout, "Good morning, Lord!" Others pull the sheet over their heads and say, "Good Lord, it's morning!"

If you are green with envy, you are ripe for trouble.

If we are to make a difference in others' lives, we have to meet them where they are.

Keep your fears to yourself, but share your courage with others.

One person's idea of keeping a secret is to refuse to divulge where they heard it.

It's a shame that alcohol doesn't turn off one's mouth at the same time it turns off one's brain.

A friend is someone who makes you feel like the person you'd like to be.

One thing for sure, flattery beats the mirror every time.

Some people don't need others to feel sorry for them. They do fine all by themselves.

The person who knows all the answers should know why she or he is unpopular.

A bore is a person who insists upon talking about himself when you want to talk about yourself.

Secrets are like sharp tools,
to be kept from the clutches of children and fools.

If you make people think they are thinking, they will love you, but if you really make them think, they will hate you.

We're not put here on this earth to see through each other, but to see each other through.

A tactless individual is one who says what everybody else is thinking.

# Friendship and Kindness

When a man is wrapped up in himself, he makes a pretty small package.

Ability gains attention, kindness gains respect.

Sometimes the best thing to get off your chest is your chin.

A victory is often shared with friends. A defeat is usually suffered alone.

Stand up to be seen.
Speak up to be heard.
Shut up to be appreciated.

The height of embarrassment is when two eyes meet at the same keyhole.

It's hard to get people to see eye-to-eye with you when you are looking down your nose at them.

It's amazing how quickly a pat on the back can lighten fatigue.

Flattery is the art of telling people what they already suspect.

I hate to repeat gossip, but what else can you do with it?

Perfect strangers cease to be perfect the minute they cease to be strangers.

Sound travels at one-fifth of a mile a second, or about the speed of a rumor.

A polite person pretends he has never heard the story before.

Character is what we are worth when nothing else counts.

In the cookies of life, friends are the chocolate chips.

Being old has its good and bad - being old and lonely is all bad.

When friends ask for a second cup, they are open to conversation.

If you wish your merit to be known, acknowledge that of other people.

A compliment is verbal sunshine.

Never apologize for showing feeling, remember that when you do so, you apologize for truth.

In prosperity, our friends know us; in adversity, we know our friends.

Friendship and Kindness

If you want people to agree with you, admit you have a fault.

Friendship is the only cement that will hold the world together.

Some grouches, have photographic memories. They remember all the negatives about their friends.

Compliments are like perfume - to be inhaled, not swallowed.

It's always a good idea to seek the advice of others, but that doesn't mean you have to take it.

People whose manners are on the absent side are probably missing more than just their manners.

When you point a finger at someone, you are pointing three at yourself.

Instead of putting others in their place, put yourself in their place.

It is better to bite your tongue than to let it bite someone else.

A gossip is a fool with a keen sense of humor.

So often our listening is only in part, what we really need is a hearing aid for the heart.

Keep good company and you will be counted among them.

The best way to spread the most news in the least time is to disguise it as a secret.

The biggest step you can take is when you meet others halfway.

Give first impressions a second opinion.

A good way to forget your troubles is to help others out of theirs.

Go often to the house of your friends, for weeds choke up the unused path.

A cheerful friend is like a sunny day.

There may be times when you will be sorry about something,
but you will never be sorry that you were kind.

Service is love in action.

# Friendship and Kindness

The only persons you should want to get even with are those who have helped you.

Sympathy says, "I'm sorry";
compassion says, "I'll help".

No time is ever wasted that makes two people better friends.

You can never win simply by trying to even the score.

What's the use of having an enemy if you can have a friend.

A friend indeed is that rare soul who sees right through us, but sees us through.

A friend is the first one to walk in when the world walks out.

A hometown is where the great are small and the small are great.

Tolerance is seeing things with your heart instead of with your eyes.

Gossip is remembered long after good deeds are forgotten.

Nobody has so little that there is no room for praise or so much that there is no need for prayer.

There is nothing as nice as a cheerful word of greeting.

Keeping a secret from some people is like trying to sneak daylight past a rooster.

Gossip is like mud thrown against a clean wall. It may stick, but it leaves a mark.

Kind words are short to speak, but their echoes are endless.

It isn't necessary to blow out the other person's light to let your own shine.

Kindness in words creates confidence.
Kindness in thinking creates profoundness.
Kindness in giving creates love.

Attitudes are contagious. Is yours worth catching?

The best way to cheer yourself up is to try to cheer somebody else up.

Praise is the soil in which joy thrives.

## Friendship and Kindness

Let your light shine with love, service, and a smile.

Criticism from a friend is better than flattery from an enemy.

Forgiveness is the key that opens the door to freedom from resentment.

A friend is long sought, hardly found, and with difficulty kept.

A gossip talks about others, a bore talks about himself, a brilliant person talks about you.

Fragrance lingers on the hands of those who hand out roses.

We find comfort among those who agree with us, growth among those who don't.

Politeness has been well-defined as benevolence in small things.

When you are good to others, you are best to yourself.

No matter what scale we use, we never know the weight of another person's burden.

Friends are those who do their knocking before they enter instead of after they leave.

Empathy is your pain in my heart.

Judge people from where they stand, not from where you stand.

Be such a person that, if all were like you, this world would be a paradise.

You never get ahead of anyone a long as you try to get even with him.

They wouldn't worry about what people think about them if they knew how seldom they do.

Before passing judgment, first treat others with courtesy, dignity, and respect.

To a friend's house the road is never long.

Help others get ahead. You will always stand tall with someone else on your shoulders.

Personality can open doors, but only character can keep them open.

# Friendship and Kindness

The opportunity for brotherhood presents itself every time you meet a human being.

There is no greater joy or greater reward than to make a fundamental difference in someone's life.

If you want others to be happy, practice compassion. If you want to be happy, practice compassion.

For the most part, fear is nothing but an illusion. When you share it with someone else it tends to disappear.

Treat your friends as you do your pictures and place them in their best light.

Nobody will believe in you unless you believe in yourself.

Keep your friends close, but keep your enemies closer.

How wise are Thy Commandments, Lord. Each one of them applies to somebody I know.

If you want to keep a friend, never suggest what's wrong with their children.

We all have the strength to endure the misfortunes of others.

There is no such thing as a secret, either it is too good to keep or not worth keeping.

Never give up on anybody. Miracles happen every day.

Your Merry Christmas may depend on what others do for you, but your happy New Year depends on what you do for others.

One nice thing about egotists: they don't talk about other people.

Kind words are the music of the world.

A good way to forget your troubles is to help others out of theirs.

Some people never get interested in anything until it's none of their business.

Before you flare up at another's faults, take time to count to 10 - of your own.

Friendship and Kindness

The quickest way to lift our living level is to lift our giving level.

Kindness, like a towel, is need at once. If you have to wait for it, you won't need it.

To keep friends, give them your candied opinion.

Kindness is not only its own reward - it usually pays dividends.

They, who always have their say, may lose some friends along the way.

The worst companion a person can find is when he flies into a rage and gets beside himself.

Nothing is as busy as an idle rumor.

Nobody has ever come up with a good substitute for friendship.

If you can't get people to listen, tell them it's confidential.

A really good friend is one who lets you be yourself - and likes you in spite of it.

Good cooks never lack friends.

Friendship fills up all those little ruts in life.

If you treat people like a doormat, they will stop showing you their WELCOME side.

The milk of human kindness has no expiration date.

People would be less likely to spill the beans if they were the ones who had to clean up the mess.

A yawn may be bad manners, but it's an honest opinion.

Cultivate kindness in all that you do and you will find kindness then cultivates you.

A secret is your slave if you keep it; your master if you lose it.

Never exchange a good conscience for the goodwill of others or to avoid their ill will.

If you're looking for friends, find those who need you.

# Friendship and Kindness

Real friendship is shown in times of trouble; prosperity is full of friends.

One's worst enemy is the one disguised as a friend.

Most people enjoy the inferiority of their best friends.

Before you begin to tell your troubles to anyone, ask yourself how you would like to listen to theirs.

We can be generous and yet not spend money. Just give a pleasant word to a discouraged person.

To speak ill of others is a dishonest way of praising ourselves.

Friendship is a two-way treat.

Never judge other people by appearances, but remember that you are always judged by them.

A good conversationalist is not one who remembers what was said, but who says what someone wants to remember.

When friends start buttering you up, you know they're going to put the bite on you.

Always listen to the opinions of others. It probably won't do you any good, but it will them.

People have a way of becoming what you encourage them to be, not what you nag them to be.

If you think it's hard to meet new people, try picking up the wrong golf ball.

A conscience is something that is more important than your neighbor's opinions.

If you like being around people who are good-natured, stick with folks who are busy.

A true friend is one soul in two bodies.

Remember others may hate you, but those who hate you don't win unless you hate them.

Most people who sing their own praises can't carry a tune.

Friendship and Kindness

Good breeding consists in concealing how much we think of ourselves and how little we think of the other person.

Every charitable act is a stepping stone toward heaven.

True friendship comes when silence between two people is comfortable.

Hating people is like burning down your own house to get rid of a rat.

Good advice is appreciated by everybody - if they are giving it.

An investment in kindness usually brings a dividend of pleasure.

Faith is assuring a friend he can do the impossible - loyalty is joining him.

Kind words, cheerful smiles, and helping hands are shafts of sunshine through clouds of sorrow.

Bigotry is the sealing wax of the mind.

Friendship is the gift of the gods, and the most precious boon to man.

A person who is a stranger to himself is the most alone of all people.

If two friends ask you to judge a dispute; don't accept, for you will lose a friend.
If two strangers ask you to judge a dispute, accept, for you will gain a friend.

If it weren't for beauty parlor gossip, some women would have to pay for group therapy.

When you run into someone who is disagreeable to others, you may be sure he is uncomfortable with himself.

The amount of pain we inflict upon others is directly proportional to the amount we feel within us.

A pat on the back develops character - if given young enough, often enough, and low enough.

If you say a bad thing, you may soon hear a worse thing said about you.

Nothing is ever lost by courtesy. It is the cheapest of the pleasures; costs nothing and conveys much. It pleases him who gives and him who receives, and thus, like mercy, is twice blessed.

# Friendship and Kindness

People who are beautiful on the outside live mostly for themselves. Those who are beautiful on the inside live mostly for others.

You don't win an argument if in the end you lose a friend.

People who write the most interesting and effective letters never answer letters; they answer people.

The person who says, "I may be wrong," is about to give you conclusive evidence that he isn't.

If you think there is some good in everybody, remember that you haven't met everybody.

A man who thinks he knows it all, is a pain in the neck to those of us who really do.

A good friend is someone who dislikes the same people you do.

Sex appeal is fifty percent what you have and fifty percent what people think you have.

It is always commendable to get in and dig, but be careful where you throw the dirt.

A good friend is somebody who could tell you about his troubles, but doesn't.

OVERHEARD: His wife's a gossip. If you can't say something nice about a person, she wants to be the first to hear it.

The best vitamin for making friends: B1.

Don't talk about yourself; it will be done when you leave.

The reason we admire persons who think before they speak is that they give us a chance to say something.

Politeness is one-half good nature and the other half good lying.

Three may keep a secret if two of them are dead.

If you aren't good at entertaining yourself, you aren't good at entertaining anyone else.

It is so easy to convert others, it is so difficult to convert oneself.

Friendship and Kindness

Morality is simply the attitude we adopt towards people whom we personally dislike.

If you are grouchy, irritable, or just plain mean, there will be a ten dollar charge for putting up with you.

My own business always bores me to death. I prefer other people's.

In matters of grave importance, style, not sincerity, is the vital thing.

If you don't anything nice to say about anybody, come sit next to me.

I always prefer to believe the best of everybody - it saves so much time.

A friend is a lot of things, but a critic he isn't.

Kind words can be short and easy to speak, but their echoes are truly endless.

If you enjoy being a guest, you must sometimes be a host.

We don't have to change friends if we understand that friends change.

Some people think they are honest because they have never been caught stealing.

If you are being run out of town, get in front of the crowd and make it look like a parade.

When you 'bury the hatchet' don't leave the handle sticking out.

Concrete, steel, and lumber make the buildings, but people make the community.

True friends are those who, when you've made a fool of yourself, don't think you've done a permanent job.

He who seeks a friend without a fault, remains without one.

He who does nothing for others does nothing for himself.

Treat arguments like weeds. Nip them in the bud.

The only people to get even with are those who have helped you.

There is a vast difference between putting your nose in other people's business and putting your heart in other people's problems.

# Friendship and Kindness

When in doubt, do the friendliest thing.

A friend is the one who comes in when the whole world has gone out.

A bore is someone who, upon leaving a room, makes you feel that someone fascinating just walked in.

Speak kind words and you will hear kind echoes.

The reward for a good deed is to have done it.

Infinite sadness is not to trust an old friend.

No one applauds the fiddle after the concert. They only applaud the fiddler. Acknowledge the fiddler in your life.

Friendship is the gold thread that ties hearts together.

Good times are easy to enjoy. The real worth of a person comes from how he acts during the bad times.

At what point does an acquaintance become a friend?

When it comes to sincerity, style is everything.

If you can't apologize, you better be good at making new friends.

A positive attitude may just annoy enough people to make it worth your while.

Always talk about others as if they were present.

The art of acceptance is the art of making someone who has just done you a small favor wish that he might have done you a greater one.

A good friend remembers what we were and sees what we can be.

If you want to make a friend, let someone do you a favor.

Personality is to man what perfume is to a flower.

God gives us relatives; thank God we can choose our friends.

You may be thinking wrong of your friend's point of view;
it isn't what you think of him but what he thinks of you.

Do unto the other feller the way he'd like to do unto you.

## Friendship and Kindness

Be too good and you will be too lonesome.

A bore deprives you of solitude and doesn't provide you with company.

To be popular, ask people for advice. Don't do anything about it, just ask.

If you can't say anything good about someone, you are about average.

You can't bring sunshine to others without splashing some on yourself.

With people and things, don't be confused - neither is yours to ever abuse.

Be pleasant to people you can't stand.

People will never completely understand you, so give them credit when they try.

Treasure your independence, but be gracious when accepting favors from others.

The people who help you move on a rainy day are true-blue friends.

Don't be so casual in dress, language, and manner that people don't take you seriously.

Don't criticize people in front of others. Nobody ever feels better.

Remember, being nice is always good business.

If you're a person who complains that nobody ever tells you anything it might be because you do tell everything.

Friends come and go, but enemies accumulate.

If you must talk about your troubles, don't bore your friends with them. Tell them to your enemies, who will be delighted to hear about them.

Judge people by their actions, not their intentions.

When someone gives you unwanted or unsolicited advice, just say, "Well that's something to think about."

Always choose character over charisma.

Virtues and values are cherished beliefs that determine behavior.

The person who doesn't gossip has no friends to speak of.

# Friendship and Kindness

Everyone you meet wears an invisible sign, it reads, "Notice me. Make me feel important."

Sometimes it's hard to comprehend who is foe and who is friend.

If you've learned that a good friend is ill, don't ask him about it, let him tell you first.

If I had to choose between betraying my country and betraying my friend, I hope I should have the guts to betray my country.

When you need professional advice, get it from professionals, not from your friends.

Ask someone you'd like to know better to list five people he would most like to meet. It will tell you a lot about him.

He who is the enemy of my enemy is my friend.

Friendship, like a young tree, must be planted in rich soil, watered with common sense to establish deep roots, and grown in the sunshine of time.

To err is human, but to blame it on someone else is even more human.

The way some people find fault, you would think there was a reward.

Nothing will stir up more mud than a groundless rumor.

The nicest thing about new friends is they haven't heard your old stories.

Promises may get friends, but it is performance that keeps them.

If you are attracted to the right kind of friends, when you start to go wrong, they will keep you going right.

Do an act of kindness every day - you will feel better for it.

"Stay" is such a charming word in a friend's vocabulary.

Refusing to ask for help when you need it is refusing someone the chance to be helpful.

Don't worry about knowing others. Make yourself worth knowing.

The time to make friends is before you need them.

Friendship and Kindness

Our duty is not to see through one another, but to see one another through.

Pleasant days are just ordinary days made better by good people.

God adds to the beauty of His world by creating true friends.

People with porches have hundreds of friends.

Keep your fears to yourself, but share your courage with others.

Forget yourself and think of others. You'll quickly find joy in life.

Hospitality means treat your company like family and your family like company.

How good it feels. . . the hand of a friend.

Deal with the faults of others as gently as with your own.

Tis much better to give than lend. All one loses is money, never friend.

Friends of people with children have to listen to the patter of little feats.

One thing you can give and still keep is your word.

It's not true that nice guys finish last. Nice guys are winners before the game even starts.

Be grateful for the doors of opportunity - and for friends who oil the hinges.

Treasure is not always a friend, but a friend is always a treasure.

If you think the world is all wrong, remember that it contains people like you.

Down in their hearts, wise men know this truth: The only way to help yourself is to help others.

Half the pleasure of crying is missed if there is nobody by to pity and comfort you.

A smile is the welcome mat at the doorway of kindness.

The best way to entertain some folks is to sit down and listen to them.

A sandwich with a friend is usually better than a steak by yourself.

True friendship is like sound health: The value of it is seldom known until it is lost.

Praise, like gold and diamonds, owes its value to its scarcity.

If you look for the best in people, it will keep you so busy you won't find time to notice the worst.

How inoffensive it is when a friend repeats himself time after time, when he is saying nice things about you.

A true friend is a work of heart.

A true friend is the greatest of all blessings, and the one which we take the least thought to acquire.

People who are sensible enough to give good advice are usually sensible enough to give none.

A person who makes people laugh secures more friends than the one who forces them to think.

Kindness is a language which the blind can read and the deaf can understand.

A true friend can hear a tear drop.

Trust is a tie that holds friendship together.

Never lie down at night without being able to say, "I have made one human being at least a little wiser, or a little happier, or at least a little better this day."

As perfume is to the flower, kindness is to speech.

Kindness, like a boomerang, always returns.

Friendship and Kindness

# Happiness and Humor

## **Happiness and Humor**

Happiness does not come from what you have, but what you are.

Grant me a sense of humor, and the saving grace to see a joke,
to win some happiness from life, and pass it along to other folk.

People who have every reason to be happy will search for one reason not to be.

Happiness stems from a loving heart.

A warm smile and wholesome laughter have great face value.

Men will take almost any kind of criticism except the observation that they have no sense of humor.

Wrinkles should merely indicate where smiles have been.

Manners are the happy way of doing things.

Happiness depends upon ourselves.

The wearer of smiles and the bearer of a kindly disposition needs no introduction, but is welcome anywhere.

Seven days without laughter makes one weak.

Humor is a social lubricant that helps us get over some of the bad spots.

Realize that true happiness lies within you.

Happiness is 25th hour after you've caught the 24 hour flu.

Anyone who is too busy to laugh is too busy.

Some people have no sense of humor,
others have no sense or humor.

Happiness is not a destination. It is a way of traveling.

We should all use our key to happiness before the lock gets rusty.

Happiness is a habit - cultivate it.

## Happiness and Humor

Delightful things are all around, simply waiting to be found.

Without laughter, life on our planet would be intolerable.

So important is laughter that societies highly reward those who make a living by inducing laughter in others.

Turn that frown upside down.

We may be sure we are not pleasing God if we are not happy ourselves.

Happiness held is a seed.
Happiness shared is a flower.

Looking at the bright side of things never hurts anyone's eyes.

Happiness is realizing after I locked the keys in the car that I also forgot to put the window up.

Happiness is having your own teeth to eat with after age seventy.

Happiness is my dog helping me finish my vegetables when mom isn't looking.

Put on a smile - one size fits all.

Laughter is the sun that drives winter from the human face.

Man is most nearly himself when he achieves the seriousness of a child at play.

The young man who has not wept is a savage; and the older man who will not laugh is a fool.

Laughter warms the home.

A smile is the carnation in the buttonhole of life.

Get happiness out of your work, or you may never know what happiness is.

Great mountains of happiness grow out of little hills of kindness.

Genuine elation comes when you feel you could touch a star without standing on tiptoe.

The gift of happiness belongs to those who unwrap it.

Happiness and Humor

The sunshine of life is made up of very little beams that are bright all the time.

A laugh is a smile that bursts.

May it matter not that we are stars, but that we twinkle.

Having a sense of humor makes it easier to get along with others - and also easier to get along with ourselves.

Never miss an opportunity to make someone happy.

I think the next best thing to solving a problem is finding some humor in it.

Between each dawn and setting sun,
set aside some time for fun.

A smile goes a long way, but usually comes back.

Unshared joy is an unlit candle.

Be happy with what you have and who you are; be generous with both, and you won't have to hunt for happiness.

Good humor is the health of the soul.

Happiness is not a station you arrive at, but a manner of traveling

If you are happy for no reason, then you are truly happy.

Fun is a minute,
joy is an hour, and
happiness is a lifetime.

The happiest man on earth is usually the one who never knows it.

Those who want it all will never know the happiness of those glad to have some of it.

Misery loves company, but happiness throws more parties.

Happiness is when my pills and pain run out at the same time.

Ecstasy is a feeling you feel when you feel you are going to feel a feeling you never felt before.

All who find joy must share it; happiness was a born twin.

Happiness is a conscious choice, not an automatic response.

Joy is the echo of God's life in us.

The groundwork of all happiness is health.

Happiness is not an absence of problems, but the ability to deal with them.

Too much of a good thing can be wonderful.

Anything you're good at contributes to happiness.

True happiness is of a retired nature, and an enemy to pomp and noise; it arises in the first place, from the enjoyment of one's self, and in the next, from the friendship and conversation of a few select companions.

Happiness is when all the children are grown and gone and you get to lick the chocolate pudding pan.

Happiness is getting your braces off a day before your junior high graduation.

The optimist is as often wrong as the pessimist, but he is much happier.

You cannot be envious and happy at the same time.

There is no happiness for people when it comes at the expense of other people.

Three essentials of happiness are: something to do, someone to love, and something to hope for.

It's important to make someone happy everyday, even if it's just yourself.

Happiness is not so much in having as in sharing.

Laughter is the brush that sweeps away the cobwebs of the heart.

Happiness is when your cat finally realizes what the litter box is for.

It isn't our position, but our disposition that makes us happy.

There can be no happiness if the things we believe in are different from the things we do.

Anything you're good at contributes to happiness.

Happiness and Humor

Laughter is like the human body wagging its tail.

Part of the happiness of life consists not in fighting battles, but in avoiding them. A masterly retreat is in itself a victory.

Be happy with what you have and who you are. Be generous with both, and you won't have to hunt for happiness.

Laughter is in the ears of the beholder.

Fun is like life insurance - the older you get, the more it costs.

Most people ask for happiness on condition. Happiness can only be felt if you don't set any condition.

One way to be happy ever after is not to be after too much.

People show their character in nothing more clearly than by what think is laughable.

If we had a job description for our lives, it would show that we should try to make others happy as well as ourselves.

A man without mirth is like a wagon without springs. He is jolted disagreeably by every pebble in the road.

Happiness is having the lab technician find your vein on the first stick.

Charm consists of laughing easily, listening intently, caring deeply, and helping frequently.

Nobody can give you a duplicate key to happiness.

It is neither wealth nor splendor, but tranquility and occupation which give happiness.

Grief can take care of itself, but to get the full value of joy you must have somebody to divide it with.

Happy people are those who are producing something.

Happiness usually depends on another human being. Satisfaction depends upon a plate of food.

A smile - it creates happiness in the home, fosters goodwill in business, and is the countersign of friends.

## Happiness and Humor

Times of sorrow are valuable - they help us recognize when we are happy.

Contempt for happiness is usually contempt for other people's happiness, and is an elegant disguise for hatred of the human race.

Happiness is finally weighing the amount that's on your driver's license.

Wit is the salt of conversation, not the food.

The easiest way to make some people happy is to just sit there and smile as you nod your head.

Laughter is not at all a bad beginning for a friendship, and it is by far the best ending for one.

One of the best things a person can have up his sleeve is a funny bone.

Success is getting what you want. Happiness is liking what you get.

You cannot hold back a good laugh any more than you can the tide, both are forces of nature.

Happiness is an inside job.

Happiness makes up in height for what it lacks in length.

Laugh hard, laugh long, laugh often and the world is yours.

There are hundreds of languages in the world, but a smile speaks all of them.

Women tend to marry men who know how to make them laugh.

Happiness is seeing your mother-in-law on a milk carton.

Laugh alone and the world thinks you're an idiot.

Those who can't laugh at themselves leave the job to others.

If you laugh and drink soda pop at the same time, it will come out your nose.

Trying to smile while saying 'soy sauce' will always make you laugh.

Learning to laugh at yourself is the surest sign of maturity.

Smile when picking up the phone. The caller will hear it in your voice.

## Happiness and Humor

Happiness is like perfume: You can't give it away without getting a little on yourself.

My way of joking is to tell the truth. It's the funniest joke in the world.

Pack up your gloomies in a box, then sit on the lid and laugh.

Smiling is contagious - frowning is outrageous.

You can choose to be happy.

Truly happy people have a profound enduring feeling of contentment and well-being.

The world is a mirror. If you smile at it, it smiles back.

Better by far you should forget and smile than that you should remember and be sad.

Happiness is helping your house guest pack to leave.

You have no more right to consume happiness without producing it than to consume wealth without producing it.

If you don't have wrinkles, you haven't laughed enough.

The best medicine is one that needs no prescription, has no unpleasant taste, and costs nothing. It's laughter.

Envy is the enemy of happiness.

A smile is something that adds to your face value.

If the problem is something you will laugh about later, why not laugh about it now?

A child's play and laughter can never be replaced.

A positive attitude is highly contagious.

When someone tells you a joke, never interrupt and say you already heard it.

Of all the things you wear, your expression is the most important.

Take time to laugh - it's the music of the soul.

# Happiness and Humor

There is no danger of developing eye strain from looking on the bright side of things.

Laughter is the spice of life.

It is impossible to be bored in the presence of a cheerful person.

If you put a smile on your face, nobody will notice the rest.

Anyone who doesn't cultivate a sense of humor may grow weeds on his disposition.

Happiness is like potato salad - the moment you share it, it becomes a picnic.

Happiness is found along the way, not at the end of the road.

A cheerful thought, like a lovely flower, can brighten any day.

Happiness is having something interesting to do, someone to love, and something to look forward to.

It's almost impossible for a person to smile on the outside without feeling better on the inside.

A laugh a day is good for the soul.

The best way to wake up with a smile on your face is to go to bed with one already there.

Happiness is the simple harmony between a man and the life he leads.

Laugh a lot - a good sense of humor cures most of life's ills.

Humor is to life what shock absorbers are to automobiles.

Recall it as often as you wish - a happy memory never wears out.

Trouble knocked at the door, heard a laugh and turned away.

Happiness and Humor

Health and Fitness

# Health and Fitness

# Health and Fitness

Good health is the thing that makes you feel that now is the best time of the year.

I did some exercise once. I got over it - I'm okay now.

How can a two pound box of candy make you gain ten pounds?

What do you do for exercise? Nothing, but I have been a pallbearer for a lot that did.

A plastic surgeon made his loved one an offer she couldn't refuse, "Marry me and you will never look a day older."

The only thing that people do that doesn't get better with practice is getting up in the morning.

Never squat with your spurs on.

What good are buns of steel, if they're attached to thighs of Jello?

Never, under any circumstances, take a sleeping pill and a laxative on the same night.

Men are like fine wine. They start out as grapes, and it's up to the women to stomp the crap out of them until they turn into something acceptable to have dinner with.

Did you hear about the dentist who married a manicurist?
Now they fight tooth and nail.

I have learned much from disease which life could have never taught me anywhere else.

If it tastes good, it must be good for you.

If you haven't any charity in your heart, you have the worst kind of heart trouble.

One of the most sublime experiences we can ever have is to wake up feeling healthy after we have been sick.

Health is the first muse, and sleep is the condition to produce it.

## Health and Fitness

A strong body makes the mind strong.

It is well to be up before daybreak, for such habits contribute to health, wealth, and wisdom.

To lengthen your life, lessen your meals.

The only way to keep your health is to eat what you don't want, drink what you don't like, and do what you'd rather not.

Never go to a doctor whose office plants have died.

I'm at the age where food has taken the place of sex in my life. In fact, I've just had a mirror put over my kitchen table.

Never lick a steak knife.

The only disability in life is a bad attitude.

If you're living in a dream world, you're a neurotic. If you make a living in a dream world, you're a psychiatrist.

It's not a diet; it's a way of life.

You cannot be fit as a fiddle if you're as tight as a drum.

If you don't take care of your body, where else are you going to live?

You don't get an ulcer from what you eat, you get an ulcer from what is eating you.

Does acupuncture cure windbags?

You know your youth has fled when you have trouble finding a doctor who looks old enough to know what he's doing.

Science has proven that nothing wears out the human body faster than doing nothing.

Did you hear about the chimney sweep, who came down with the flu?

The only reason I would take up jogging is so I could hear heavy breathing again.

What's the most fattening thing you can put in a banana split?
Your spoon.

Health and Fitness

People who cough a lot never seem to go to doctors. They go to movies instead.

High priced doctors and huge hospital fees make it impossible to be ill at ease.

Curious isn't it? The thinner your hair gets, the thicker your waist gets.

If you look like your passport photo, you are too ill to travel.

By the time I'm thin, fat will be in.

I try to watch what I eat, but my eyes aren't always fast enough.

When I said I learned to live with a pain in the neck, I was talking about my husband.

By the time a man can afford to hire someone to cut the grass, his doctor tells him he needs the exercise.

The doctor said you will regain use of everything but your money.

Following his annual physical, a man asked for the results. His doctor said, "The examination revealed one important thing. You wear cute polka-dot shorts."

I'm on three different diets at the same time - it's the only way I get enough to eat.

Times change - bullies no longer kick sand in the face of the weak ninety-pound weakling, they ask him for his diet.

The secret to dieting is not to eat between snacks.

"Hey Doc, you sure kept your promise when you said you would have me walking again in a month.
"Well, that's fine."
"Yes, I had to sell my car when I got your bill."

Two six-year olds were talking. One said, "Let's play doctor. You operate and I'll sue."

I'd give up chocolate, but I'm no quitter.

No matter how much you pay for a private hospital room, you are still going to get a semiprivate gown.

# Health and Fitness

To men a twenty-mile hike is physical fitness. To women it's called shopping.

Hypochondriac's headstone: "I told you I was sick."

Running late seems to be the only exercise I have time for.

Why diet, getting into Heaven isn't going to depend on the size of your waistline.

If you want to look young and thin, hang out with old, fat people.

Even when freshly washed and relieved of all confections, children tend to be sticky.

Exercise is a dirty word. Every time I hear it, I wash my mouth out with chocolate.

No one becomes dizzy from doing good turns.

I have such a great doctor. If you can't afford the operation, he touches up the X-rays.

Eating your words comes after your biting remarks.

Anything consumed while standing has no calories. This is due to gravity and the density of the caloric mass.

One result of working day and night is you'll earn enough to pay the hospital bill.

A physician's duty is not just to extend life; it's also to end suffering.

Enthusiasm is like measles: If you don't have it, you can't give it to anyone.

Grief is itself a medicine.

When you have to swallow your own medicine, the spoon always seems about three times as big.

The best exercise for the heart is to bend down and help someone.

Get on your knees and thank God you're on your feet.

Every man must walk in the garden of his soul.

## Health and Fitness

I knew a man who gave up smoking, drinking, sex, and food. He was healthy right up to the time he killed himself.

Envy eats nothing, but its own heart.

Did you hear about the patient who was being fed intravenously? He asked the doctor for an extra bottle. He was having a guest for lunch.

Everybody needs a hug. It changes your metabolism.

No matter how much you nurse a grudge it won't get better.

My doctor said I was sound as a dollar and that scared the hell out of me.

If you're pushing fifty, that's exercise enough.

Sometimes we all feel like a snapdragon - no snap and everything draggin'.

You have to know what's biting you before you reach for a remedy.

After forty, life is just a physical maintenance job.

Two things are bad for the heart - running up hills and running down people.

A worry a day drains vitality away.

The only kind of painless dentistry is the kind practiced on someone else.

When you hide your emotions, your stomach keeps score.

The person who gives you a detailed account of his operation makes you experience the pain without the benefit of anesthesia.

Hardening of the heart is worse than hardening of the arteries.

Some folks think we'll live longer if we give up everything that makes us want to.

These days, a miracle drug is one that is sold at an affordable price.

The race may not always go to the swift, but it does always go to one of the runners.

Advice is like medicine; you have to take it to find out if it does you any good.

# Health and Fitness

About the only exercise some people get is running down coworkers, sidestepping responsibilities, and pushing their luck.

A recent survey found that nine out of ten doctors say, "Do you have insurance?"

On-and-off dieters are people who fluctuweight.

Another great medical breakthrough would be the discovery that a patient's time is worth something.

Advice after injury is like medicine after death.

You know a woman is a serious dieter when she starts taking off her makeup before getting on the scale.

We would have a very poor appearance if the scars on our souls showed.

Watch out for fake medical cures. When you see a quack, duck.

There is far more hunger for love and appreciation in the world than there is hunger for bread.

Moderation is a fatal thing, nothing succeeds like excess.

It's a good thing that life isn't all peaches and cream. We would have to watch out for the pits and cholesterol.

People who are late for doctor appointments are usually right on time.

We should always keep in mind that cutting remarks have a way of leaving scars.

At my age, all I exercise is caution.

Show me a person with a bad toothache and I'll show you a person who's dentally disturbed.

Those who misbehave know that time wounds all heels.

If you don't take care of your body, where else are you going to live?

Part of the secret of success in life is to eat what you like and let the food fight it out inside.

Many a man's tongue has broken his nose.

# Health and Fitness

Of all the home remedies, a good wife is still the best.

Anything consumed from someone else's plate has no calories, since the calories rightfully belong to the other person.

You cannot be fit as a fiddle if you are as tight as a drum.

If you cannot read the writing, there's a good chance that it was written by a doctor telling the pharmacist, "I've got mine, now you get yours."

The wound of a sword will heal; the wound of a tongue will not.

You must work seven days a week, ten hours each day, if you intend to pay for your heart attack.

You always gain five pounds on the scale at the doctor's office.

Overweight is hereditary - it shows up in your jeans.

The day you begin a diet, someone wants to take you to dinner in your favorite restaurant.

Seeing is deceiving, it's eating that's believing.

My doctor told me I had low blood pressure, so he gave me my bill that raised it.

A diet is the penalty we pay for exceeding the food limit.

When someone asks, "How are you doing?" It's not necessary to give them a full health report.

I read this article that said the typical symptoms of stress are eating too much, drinking too much, impulse buying, and driving too fast. Are they kidding? That is my idea of a perfect day.

It's a little too much to save, and a little too much to dump.
There's nothing to do, but eat it, that makes a person plump.

Cookie pieces contain no calories. The process of breaking causes calorie leakage.

Things licked off of knives and spoons have no calories, if you are in the process of preparing something.

If God had wanted me to touch my toes, he would have put them on my knees.

# Health and Fitness

Good health is merely the slowest possible rate at which one can die.

Don't look forward to the day you stop suffering, because when it comes, you will know you're dead.

I get enough exercise just pushing my luck.

I didn't fight my way to the top of the food chain to be a vegetarian.

When you eat with someone else, calories don't count if you do not eat more than they do?

The severity of the itch is inversely proportional to the ability to reach it.

Why did the doctor keep his bandages in the refrigerator?
He wanted to use them for cold cuts.

If you drink a diet soda with a candy bar, the calories in the candy bar are canceled out by the diet soda.

If you eat something and no one sees you eat it, it has no calories.

Food used for medicinal purposes never count, such as hot chocolate?

Forget the pain and get on with the party.

Temptation is sure to ring your doorbell, but do not ask it to stay for dinner.

The better the doctor, the harder it is to read his or her handwriting.

Chocolate is a food group.

My doctor is a family physician, he treats my family, and I support his.

I am a light eater. I eat everything in sight as soon as it is light.

When mom is on a diet, everyone's on a diet.

Never inhale through your nose when eating a powdered doughnut.

If they don't have chocolate in Heaven, I am not going.

If you want breakfast in bed, sleep in the kitchen.

Doctors say that if you eat slowly, you will eat less. Anybody raised in a large family will tell you the same thing.

## Health and Fitness

Some schools enforce a strict rule on sports; No athlete is awarded a letter unless he can tell which letter it is.

Dinner is ready when the smoke alarm goes off.

If it doesn't bleed, you won't get much sympathy.

I don't take accidents personally - like the Mafia, it's just business.

Never buy clothes with the idea that you will lose weight.

Things would be worse - sex could be fattening.

Never take oats lightly.

Stress is what happens when your gut says no, and your mouth says, yes, I will be glad to.

Never drive faster than your angel can fly.

I finally got my head together, now my body is falling apart.

Funny, I don't remember being absent-minded.

If you don't think there is a devil, when on a diet, try getting past his cake.

By the time I'm thin, fat will be in.

I never feel lonely in the kitchen. Food is very friendly.

The most tiring exercise in the world is carrying yesterday on your back.

People who had operations often give organ recitals.

Cupcakes are served without handles.

Gardening is something that is healthy exercise if you can straighten up afterward.

If the cake has your name on it, it has no calories.

Even when I have pains, I don't have to be a pain.

If you like garlic, salt, and Tabasco sauce, you can make almost anything taste good.

# Health and Fitness

Whatever you go to the doctor for, it feels better once you get there.

If the peanut butter and jelly don't leak out of the sandwich, there's not enough peanut butter and jelly on it.

As long as I have my health, older is better than younger.

There's a new Chinese diet: You eat your food with one chopstick.

Swallow your pride - it is non-fattening.

Walking is a popular form of exercise that loses some appeal when it is done behind a lawn mower.

God's crumbs are better than the world's loaves.

The trouble with jogging is that by the time you realize you're not in shape for it, it's too far to walk back.

Some people think that a balanced diet is a burger in each hand.

You never realize what a poor loser you are until you start dieting.

If God intended us to eat peanut butter, the roof of our mouth would be Teflon coated.

Maintaining good health would be a breeze if oatmeal tasted as good as bacon.

Eating lots of fiber will make you a bran new person.

A diet is the penalty we pay for exceeding the feed limit.

Today the four basic food groups are too fat, too salty, too tasteless, and too expensive.

I'm tired of all this nonsense about beauty being only skin-deep. That's deep enough. What do you want - an adorable pancreas?

When a hypochondriac has the measles, he tells you how many.

He who has health has hope, and he who has hope, has everything.

If you want to look like a picture of health, you need to have a good frame of mind.

Health and Fitness

# *Adversity*

## **Adversity**

You can't make an omelet without breaking a few eggs.

Persistence prevails when all else fails.

Of all the troubles great or small, the greatest are those that don't happen at all.

If you want a place in the sun, you have to put up with a few blisters.

If you understand the problem, it isn't a problem.

The difference between the impossible and the possible lies in a person's determination.

A setback is the opportunity to begin again more intelligently.

Every exit is an entrance somewhere else.

Keep your mind on the objective, not the obstacle.

Dread, once conquered, means a victory won.

Adversity reveals genius; prosperity conceals it.

The more difficult the obstacle, the stronger one becomes after hurdling it.

There is never any great loss without some small gain.

Bad is never good, until worse happens.

It's not the load that breaks you down, it's how you carry it.

Obstacles are what you see when you take your eyes off your goal.

When you are up to your ears in trouble, try using the part that is not submerged.

If the wind doesn't blow, row.

Worry is nothing more than a mental picture of something that you don't want to happen.

# Adversity

Half of what you worry about never happens, and the other half happens for the best.

If you stumble twice over the same stone, you deserve to fall.

Many strokes overthrow the tallest oaks.

A seedling must weather many a storm before it becomes an oak.

You can't get to the end of something until you get to the middle of it.

Real difficulties can be overcome - it's the imaginary ones that are unconquerable.

God put a tear in your eye so that you could see a rainbow.

It isn't the mountains ahead that wear you out; it's the grain of sand in your shoe.

If the worst that can happen has happened, cheer up. It's the worst that can happen.

You can not raise anything if you don't raise a little sweat.

Murphy's second law: When things can't possibly get any worse, they will.

Remember, it at first you don't succeed, you're in the majority.

Stumbling blocks and stepping stones are different only in the way people use them.

The news may be bad, but it soon becomes old and is easily forgotten.

Stressed spelled backwards is desserts.

A diamond is a chunk of coal that made good under pressure.

Nothing great was ever done without much enduring.

The greatest test of courage on earth is to bear defeat without losing heart.

Over every mountain is a path that can't be seen from the valley.

A man who kneels can stand up to anything.

A weed is no more than a flower in disguise.

Adversity

Problems are only opportunities with thorns on them.

We are all faced with a series of great opportunities brilliantly disguised as impossible situations.

A man is not finished when he is defeated. He is finished when he quits.

One thorn of experience is worth a whole wilderness of warning.

There is a belief that trouble builds character, but most people would rather have less trouble and swap character for happiness.

God will either lighten you load or strengthen your back.

If you can find a path with no obstacles, it probably doesn't lead anywhere.

That which is bitter to endure may be sweet to remember.

In the middle of difficulty lies opportunity.

It never works to drown your sorrows. They are the best swimmers in the world.

Tenacity makes up for a little shortage of talent.

If dandelions were hard to grow, they would be welcome on any lawn.

To see what is in front of one's nose requires a constant struggle.

If you have a job without any problems, you don't have much of a job.

A gem cannot be polished without friction, nor the man perfected without trials.

Always prepare a plan B.

The size of your troubles generally depends on whether they are coming or going.

We need some clouds in our life to have a beautiful sunset.

Never let the seeds keep you from enjoying the watermelon.

# Success and Failure

## Success and Failure

Success isn't permanent, and failure isn't fatal.

Most rules for success won't work unless you do.

It's a lot better to stumble than not to take the first step.

Persisting with what you think is right, when others disagree, is the basis of all progress.

There is a close connection between getting up in the world and getting up in the morning.

Success comes in cans;
failure in can'ts.

Work is something that when we have it we wish we didn't; when we don't have it we wish we did, and the object is to be able to afford not to do any someday.

To believe a thing impossible is to make it so.

Stress is what happens when your gut says no and your mouth says, "Yes, I'd be glad to."

The more a man ridicules something, the more he fears it.

If two people on a committee agree on absolutely everything, one of them is unnecessary.

If you can't dream it, you can't do it.

The best cure for envy is to take over your boss's job in an emergency.

Establishing goals is all right if you don't let them deprive you of interesting detours.

Little strokes fell great oaks.

Failure is a far better teacher than success, but she hardly ever finds apples on her desk.

Never be afraid to try something new. Remember that a lone amateur built the ark and a large group of professionals built the Titanic.

## Success and Failure

We must find our duties in what comes to us. Not in what might have been.

Don't look back, somebody may be gaining on you.

There are many ways of going forward, but only one way of standing still.

Whoever wants to reach a distant goal must take many small steps.

He that can have patience can have what he will.

Always listen to experts. They'll tell you what can't be done and why. Then do it.

Meetings are indispensable when you don't want to do anything.

"If" and "when" were planted and "nothing" grew.

Use what talents you possess. The woods would be very silent if no birds sang there except those that sang best.

Luck is a matter of preparation meeting opportunity.

Expecting success without hard work is like trying to harvest where you haven't planted.

In order to succeed, we must first believe that we can.

The highest reward for a person's toil is not what they get for it, but what they become by it.

Sweet is the cologne of accomplishment.

Discoveries are often made by not following instructions, by going off the main road, and by trying the untried.

He who conquers others is strong; he who conquers himself is mighty.

Even if you're on the right track, you'll get run over if you just sit there.

Diligence is the mother of good luck.

Always bear in mind that your own resolution to succeed is more important than any other one thing.

Forget past mistakes. Forget failures, forget everything except what you are going to do now, and do it.

Success and Failure

A six word formula for success: think things through - then follow through.

Aim high. There is little virtue in easy victory.

Success is going from failure to failure without loss of enthusiasm.

The vision must be followed by the venture. It is not enough to stare up the steps, we must step up the stairs.

The journey is the reward.

I don't know the key to success, but the key to failure is trying to please everybody.

I do know that I am responsible not for what happens, but what I make of it.

You miss a hundred percent of the shots you never take.

One of the surest ways to kill off a good idea is to do nothing but entertain it.

It never gets cooked unless you put it on the burner.

It is a great piece of skill to know how to guide your luck even while you're waiting for it.

Action springs not from thought, but from readiness for responsibility.

If there is any possibility of something going wrong, it will be the thing that costs the most to fix.

If you are sure everything will be OK, you've just overlooked something.

Show me a good loser and I'll show you a born loser.

A man would do nothing if he waited until he could do it so well that no one could find fault.

Clearing away cobwebs does no good unless you get the spider.

There is one redeeming thing about a mistake. . . it proves that somebody stopped talking long enough to do something.

Form follows function, presentation is everything.

## Success and Failure

If you don't know where you are going, you will probably end up someplace else.

The secret of success is constancy of purpose.

If you start off on the wrong foot, you are out of step the rest of the way.

Life is a succession of lessons enforced by immediate reward, or more often, by immediate chastisement.

He who considers his work beneath him will be doing it well.

Look round the habitable world. How few know their own good, or knowing it, pursue.

Fate leads the willing and drags along the reluctant.

No amount of advance planning will ever replace dumb luck, but dumb luck will only take you so far - and then you had better have something else going for you.

A new broom sweeps clean, but the old broom knows the corners.

Success is a journey, not a destination.

The man who halted on third base to congratulate himself failed to make a homerun.

Solutions occur when we think things out.
Worries occur when we think things in.

One way to get ahead and stay ahead is to use your head.

Even a fish would avoid trouble if he kept his mouth shut.

If you don't know where you are going, you have already arrived.

Look forward to some success, not backward to any failure.

Always take hold of things with a smooth handle.

The easiest way to improve your luck is to stop betting.

Don't only do what you like to do, but learn to like what has to be done.

You are most efficient when you deliberately forget what is unimportant.

## Success and Failure

Ask God's blessings on your work, but don't ask Him to do it for you.

Work is work only when you'd rather be doing something else.

The bee that gets the honey doesn't hang around the hive.

The difficult we do today; the impossible takes a little longer.

Those who roll up their sleeves seldom lose their shirts.

Some people think they are overworked because it takes them all day to do a half day's work.

The person who wakes up and finds himself a success hasn't been asleep.

Every calling is great when greatly pursued.

A man who is waiting for something to turn up should start with his own sleeves.

Nothing is impossible for the man who doesn't have to do it himself.

The greatest reward for doing good is the opportunity to do more.

In you, which is stronger - success thoughts or failure thoughts.

The reward of a thing well done is having it done.

One thing worse than making a mistake is to discover you're so unimportant that nobody noticed it.

One disadvantage with having nothing to do is you can't stop and rest.

Pick your rut carefully, for you may be in it for a long time.

The best way to dress for success is to put work clothes on your hopes and dreams.

Hope for perfection, but don't scorn improvement.

Winners are self-confident, losers are self-centered;
winners are self-disciplined, losers are self-destructive.

Knowing what to do is important, but never more important than knowing what not to do.

Those who learned from experience say that the quickest way to do things is do only one thing at a time.

You'll never get out of a rut by spinning your wheels.

Sometimes choosing the lesser of two evils is nothing more than giving up the search for yet another way.

The worst inadequacy is failure to recognize our own inadequacies.

You always pass failure on the way to success.

Winners become what they can be;
losers succumb to mediocrity.

Much of success is doing what you should do rather than what you want to do.

Goals without time limits are only wishes.

If you think bigger is always better, try to remember the last time you had a toothache.

Good-luck is a lazy man's estimate of a worker's success.

State-of-the-art automation will never beat the waste basket when it comes to speeding up efficiency in the office.

Dress a little better than your clients, but not as well as your boss.

Hit or miss methods usually miss.

Never criticize the person who signs your paycheck. If you are unhappy with your job, resign.

If you have a hill to climb, waiting won't make it smaller.

Following the line of least resistance makes men, women, and rivers crooked.

The best way to make a fire with two sticks is to be sure one of them is a match.

"When in doubt, do nothing?" Apparently some people doubt everything. Nothing succeeds like failure.

Success and Failure

You can send a message around the world in one seventh of a second, yet it may take years to move a simple idea through a quarter inch of human skull.

A winner says, "Let's find out."
A loser says, "Nobody knows."

Bad habits are like a comfortable bed - easy to get into, but hard to get out of.

The trouble with quitting is that you will never know how close you came to succeeding.

No one can make you feel inferior without your consent.

The man who wins may have been counted out several times, but he didn't hear the referee.

Any failure will tell you success is nothing but luck.

Only a fool tests the depth of the water with both feet.

Great opportunities to help others seldom come, but small ones surround us daily.

Nothing great was ever achieved without enthusiasm.

If your ship doesn't come in, swim out to it.

If a window of opportunity appears, don't pull down the shade.

What would life be if we had no courage to attempt?

He who never made a mistake never made a discovery.

Truly nothing is to be expected, but the unexpected.

There is no room at the top for those who ought to start near the bottom.

When nothing can be done about a problem, you've overlooked something.

Luck is a matter of preparation meeting opportunity.

Victory belongs to the player who makes the next-to-last mistake.

The loser blames the target when he misses.
The winner adjusts his sights and aims again.

## Success and Failure

Always play the hand you were dealt as though the guys with better hands will fold.

A single reason why you can do something is worth a hundred reasons why you can't.

What is the use of running when we are not on the right road?

If you can't take God with you, don't go.

When things go wrong, don't go with them.

No opportunity is ever lost. Someone else seizes the ones you missed.

The pessimist finds the worst in the best;
the optimist discovers the best in the worst.

Never cry so loud about your hard luck that you can't hear opportunity knocking.

When opportunity knocks, a pessimist complains about the noise.

Maybe the reason so many folks have their backs to the wall is that they have been putting up too much of a front.

To know how to refuse is as important as to know how to consent.

Every idea has its doubters; every accomplishment, its critics.

Success comes from what you think, not what you think you ought to do.

People succeed only when they've been granted the right to fail.

Always give a hundred percent and you'll never have to second-guess yourself.

You may be disappointed if you fail, but you are doomed if you don't try.

Many of us would like to move mountains, but few of us are willing to practice on small hills.

Things may come to those who wait, but only the things left by those who hustle.

You can pull on a duck's neck all you want, but you're still not going to come up with a swan.

## Success and Failure

Be not afraid of moving slowly; be afraid of standing still.

Go the extra mile - it makes a mile of difference.

Most of us act experienced when we are really looking for something else.

Don't expect too much from the man who talks about what he did instead of what he's doing.

Opportunities always look bigger going away than coming.

When you reach for the stars you may not quite get one, but you won't come up with a handful of mud either.

I've always tried to go a step past wherever people expected me to end up.

I have never seen a monument erected to a pessimist.

Some people go through life bunting - never enjoying the thrill of hitting a home run.

Opportunity doesn't come - it has always been there.

Self-discipline is when your conscience tells you to do something and you don't talk back.

Nothing is easy to the unwilling.

The only way to discover the limits of the possible is to go beyond them to the impossible.

Lose as if you like it; win as if you were used to it.

If you are searching for a rich plot of ground to cultivate, don't overlook the vast territory in your head.

Throw away the bad experience, but save the lesson.

If you smile when everything goes wrong, you're either a nitwit or a repairman.

Not everything that is faced can be changed, but nothing can be changed until it is faced.

Every exit is an entry somewhere.

The time to repair the roof is when the sun is shining.

# Success and Failure

Successful people work through unpleasant tasks by looking ahead.

Don't waste time waiting for inspiration. Begin and inspiration will find you.

Don't wait for something to turn up; get a spade and dig for it.

The best job goes to the person who can get it done without passing the buck or coming back with excuses.

The man who gets ahead is the one who does more than is necessary.

On the edge of a precipice, only a fool does cartwheels.

As you slide down the banister if life, don't get a splinter in your career.

Doing business without advertising is like winking at a girl in the dark - you know what you are doing, but nobody else does.

Why not go out on a limb? That's where all the fruit is.

Knowing is not enough; we must apply.
Willing is not enough; we must do.

The Lord did not burden us with work; He blessed us with it.

When things start going your way, it's usually you who have changed directions.

The world is full of willing people - some willing to work, the rest willing to let them.

It takes backbone, not wishbone to make success.

Enthusiasm is the yeast that raises a lot of dough.

Success is never final, and failure is never fatal; it is courage that counts.

It is better to deserve honors and not have them, than to have them and not deserve them.

Procrastination is opportunity's natural assassin.

Success is the maximum utilization of the ability that you have.

Fear of change causes some persons to be
comfortable in their misery,

## Success and Failure

secure in their mediocrity and
paralyzed in their prejudice.

Rather fail with honor than succeed by fraud.

Nothing in the world can take the place of persistence.

If at first you don't succeed, try reading the manual.

Enthusiasm is the mother of effort, and without it nothing great is accomplished.

When we pray to Heaven for something, it seems to be more effective if we work like hell.

Rust ruins more tools than does overuse.

A goal is a dream with a deadline.

There is no surer way to uncover luck than opening your eyes and rolling up your sleeves.

Apologies and excuses are sometimes appropriate, but they are never adequate substitutes for thorough preparation and wise action.

You can always tell when you're on the right road - it's uphill.

Goal-setters are seldom clock-watchers;
winners are rarely whiners,
champions are never cheaters.

Mishaps are like knives that either serve us or cut us, as we grasp them by the blade or the handle.

The easiest way to catch a train is by waiting for it.

The secret to success is to do what is right over and over again.

An inventor seldom is the first person who had the idea; he's just the first one to do the required work.

Some people are like blisters, they don't show up until the work is done.

Winners never quit and quitters never win.

Rejecting all new ideas will save you a lot of headaches and any hope of progress.

# Success and Failure

If what you had to do to win bothers you, the victory is not complete.

A good way to knock the chip off a co-worker's shoulder is to pat him on the back.

Show me a man who can smile when something goes wrong and I'll show you a man who has someone to blame it on.

When life throws you a curve, remember that one move can turn it into a home run.

The winner sees a green near every sand trap;
the loser sees sand traps near every green.

Running a risk is often safer than running from it.

Ability is not a rarity. What is rare, is a person who makes use of his ability.

A person is average only so long as he can see the other fellow's faults; he becomes above average when he can also see his own.

Broad-mindedness enables you to see both sides of a problem, but not necessarily the solution.

I have never heard of anyone achieving success by doing work he didn't like to do.

I am a great believer in luck, and I find the harder I work the more I have of it.

The squeaky wheel doesn't always get greased; sometimes it gets replaced.

Why is it that some people are always quick to condemn that which they cannot do?

Snowflakes are one of nature's most fragile things, but look at what they can do when they stick together.

Success is something that always comes faster to the man your wife almost married.

Every calling is great when greatly pursued.

Everyone has a fair turn to be as great as he pleases.

Success and Failure

Consider the postage stamp: It secures success through its ability to stick to one thing until it gets there.

Shallow men believe in luck, strong men in cause and effect.

Most of us take the limits of our own field of vision for the limits of the world.

You have to know the ropes in order to pull the strings.

Courage is fighting on, even if you have no plans of how you are going to handle the victory.

You'll never plow a field by turning it over in your mind.

An optimist is one who takes cold water thrown upon his idea, heats it with enthusiasm, and uses the steam to push ahead.

The rooster crows, but the hen delivers.

Before you criticize some of the odd folks you work with, remember that to build a really great machine you need a few nuts.

I love deadlines; I especially like the whooshing sound they make as they go flying by.

Diligence is the mother of good luck.

The person, who has a right to boast, doesn't have to.

One of the hardest things about the business of life is minding your own.

To make a long story short, there's nothing like having the boss walk in during the middle of it.

There's no need to fear the wind if your haystacks are tied down.

Find a job you love and you will never have to work a day in your life.

Eighty percent of success is showing up.

Nothing is so embarrassing as watching someone do something that you said couldn't be done.

There are no shortcuts to any place worth going.

If you are not part of the solution, then you are part of the problem.

# Success and Failure

Champions keep playing until they get it right.

Dreams are where you want to go; work is how you get there.

Many a man, who is offered the chance of a lifetime for a song, can't sing.

When you turn green with envy, you're getting ripe for trouble.

You never get the chance to be lucky unless you take risks.

The early bird may get the worm, but the second mouse gets the cheese.

To question opinions is wise; to quarrel with facts is foolish.

Slow witted is when your gut feeling says no and your mouth says, "Yes, I will chair that committee."

Success always occurs in private and failure in full view.

The will to win is not nearly as important as the will to prepare to win.

Opportunity is usually where you were and not where you are.

Things work out best for those who make the best of the way things work out.

An admission of error is a sign of strength rather than a weakness.

It's not where we are that counts, it's what direction we are moving.

Fall seven times. Stand up eight.

While you're standing there deciding whether or not to get your net, the butterfly is flying away.

Not losing does not constitute a viable strategy.

Sometimes there is gain without pain.

The key is in having a destination, a flight plan, and a compass.

No other personal quality contributes to success more than persistence in the pursuit of one's goals.

If opportunity doesn't knock, build a door.

## Success and Failure

When you are problem minded, you want to eliminate something. When you are opportunity minded, you want to bring something into existence.

To win without risk is to triumph without glory.

The way to secure success is to be more anxious about obtaining it than about deserving it.

The pessimist sees problems as difficulties and complains, "Ow!"
The optimist accepts problems as challenges and exclaims, "Wow!"

What helps a person succeed is someone who expects him to.

There is only one success - to be able to spend your life in your own way.

Ambition makes more trusty slaves than needed.

The person you would most hate to lose to, will always be the one who beats you.

Second place is the first loser.

When you are all out of brilliance, dazzle them with enthusiasm.

Opportunity always knocks at the least opportune moment.

If it's worth doing, do it right away. Good intentions don't store well.

The first thing to try when all else fails, is again.

If you think you can win, you can win. Faith is necessary to victory.

Make your point, but don't stick anyone with it.

Admit you are wrong when you are wrong and you will be all right.

If you don't do any more than you get paid for you will never get paid for any more than you do.

Never be afraid to tackle a job too big or too small.

Bet on the fellow who expects to win, not the one who simply wants to.

Try doing for yourself before you ask for help.

If your life is free of failures, you are not taking enough risks.

## Success and Failure

An optimist thinks that this is the best possible world.
A pessimist fears that's true.

Don't let complaining give you more satisfaction than taking action.

It is better to know some of the questions than all the answers.

Sometimes there is gain without pain.

If you're going to be a failure, at least be one at something you enjoy.

Being willing is far more important than being able.

When in doubt, mumble,
when in trouble, delegate.

Insure your success by doing common things uncommonly well.

Progress is like a jet plane; Fly with it, or stand on the runway and risk getting blown away.

If you have enough push, you don't need any pull.

He who builds according to every man's advice will have a crooked house.

Busy hands are happy hands.

The secret to success in business is surprisingly simple: Give people more than they expect and do it cheerfully.

Enthusiasm and success just seem to go together.

It's a lot easier to object to the way things are being done than it is to do them better yourself.

He who has known defeat without losing heart has encountered victory.

If the blind lead the blind, both shall fall into the ditch.

There's a big difference between keeping your chin up and sticking your neck out.

If you are satisfied with a pound, you will never have a ton.

If you can't work and talk at the same time, better to keep your mouth closed.

Success and Failure

The road to success is dotted with many tempting parking places.

Don't mistake the ladder of success for an escalator.

The person who takes responsibility on his shoulders is not likely to have a chip there.

Coming together is a beginning;
keeping together is progress;
staying together is success.

The only thing you can get for nothing is failure.

Nothing splendid has ever been achieved except by those who dared believe something inside them was superior to circumstance.

Take your work seriously, but yourself lightly.

You cannot enjoy the harvest without first laboring in the fields.

Neglecting your work will make you despise it
Doing it well, you will enjoy, even prize it.

Success has a simple formula - do your best and people may like it.

It is better to look ahead and prepare than to look back and regret.

Anybody can grab a tiger by the tail. You only survive by knowing what to do next.

You succeed in this world if you're a self-starter, keep your motor running and know when to step on the gas.

There is no great success without great commitment.

When there is work to be done, turn up your sleeves, not your nose.

A man who has committed a mistake and does not correct it has committed another mistake.

Do not wait for your ship to come in if you haven't sent one out.

Always aim for achievement and forget about success.

Success is knowing the difference between cornering people and getting them in your corner.

Success does to living what sunshine does to stained glass.

Talent is like a picture taken by a camera - to amount to anything, it needs developing.

If we try and fail, we have temporary disappointment.
If we don't try, we have permanent regret.

In a difficult enterprise, the best backing you can have is a stiff spine.

Success is not the result of spontaneous combustion; you must first set yourself on fire.

Where and when we cannot invent, we may at least improve.

On your way up the ladder of success watch out for the person behind you.

Judge your success by the degree that you're enjoying peace, health, and love.

Success comes to the person who does today what you were thinking of doing tomorrow.

Optimists are often as wrong as pessimists, but they have a lot more fun.

Co-operation, not competition, is the life of business.

When someone else blows your horn, the sound carries twice as far.

For the resolute and determined there is time and opportunity.

People who do things that count never stop to count them.

Today's preparation determines tomorrow's achievement.

Success is often one idea away.

A man is not finished when he is defeated. He is finished when he quits.

Success and Failure

# *Life*

## Life

Live life with intensity.

Life is like a ladder, every step we take is either up or down.

Life is a tragedy to those who feel, but a comedy to those who think.

We make a living by what we get; we make a life by what we give.

If life seems like its all uphill, you must be reaching your peak.

Knowing how to make a living is important, but never as important as knowing how to live.

Next to knowing when to seize an opportunity, the most important thing in life is to know when to forgo an advantage.

To avoid criticism, do nothing, say nothing, be nothing.

One nice thing about living alone, all the decisions are unanimous.

It is a funny thing about life. If you refuse to accept anything but the best, you very often get it.

Loneliness doesn't tell you what you have lost, only that something is missing.

Being a survivor has to mean more than just staying alive.

Change is not really an optional thing.

Accept that some days you're the pigeon, and some days you're the statue.

Words are plentiful, but deeds are precious.

We all take different paths in life, but no matter where we go, we take a little of each other everywhere.

Hot heads and cold hearts never solved anything.

Never drive faster than your angel can fly.

There are only two shoulders you can rely on, and they both belong to you.

It matters not how a man dies, but how he lives.

One of the secrets of a happy life is continuous small treats.

Health is the greatest gift,
contentment the greatest wealth,
faithfulness the best relationship.

Life is like riding a bicycle - you don't fall off unless you stop pedaling.

It's alright letting yourself go as long as you can let yourself back.

Life is too marvelous, too brimming with color for me to get tired.

Attitude is everything, that's what will determine the quality of your life.

Learn to listen; opportunity may be knocking at your door very softly.

There is more to life than increasing its speed.

Having the right aim in life isn't enough if you run out of ammunition.

The trouble with life is you're halfway through it before you realize it's a do-it-yourself project.

The secret of life is not to do what you like, but to like what you do.

You have to take life as it happens, but you should try to make it happen the way you want to take it.

Learn the joy of giving. . . for when you only receive you miss much of life.

If you never have a dream, you will never have a dream come true.

Choice, not chance, determines destiny.

If you want to leave footprints in the sands of time, don't drag your feet.

Contentment is contagious.

The most effective water power in the world is tears.

Most of the mountains we climb in life we build ourselves.

Life's heaviest burden is to have nothing to carry.

# Life

Life is no better if we worry;
life is no better if we hurry.

As long as we are changing, we are living.

The secret to enjoying your life is to count your blessings - not your birthdays.

The Golden Rule has no inches or feet, yet it is the measure of every man.

The greatest wastes in life are untried ideas and unused talents.

Miracles, when aided and abetted by determined action, do happen.

Gray hairs are a glorious crown which is worn by a righteous life.

More often than we realize, what we didn't achieve, we didn't want.

The trouble with living alone is that it is always your turn to do the dishes.

One of the toughest lessons in life is learning to expect the unexpected.

Man is in possession of his own life when he can control his thoughts, rule his passions, and govern his habits.

People who rush through life shouldn't be too surprised if they get to the end a little sooner than anticipated.

When opportunity knocks on your door, you cannot possibly open it if you remain lying on the couch.

Don't ever give people a chance to reach any conclusion about you, but the one you want.

Fear of change causes some persons to be:
comfortable in their misery,
secure in their mediocrity, and
paralyzed in their prejudice.

Don't worry about other people making a fool of you. That's strictly a do-it-yourself project.

It's not about where you're going. It's about what you leave behind.

Some people are born mediocre,
some people achieve mediocrity, and
some people have mediocrity thrust upon them.

We are confronted with insurmountable opportunities.

After all is said and done, no matter how famous or important a man may be, the size of his funeral is going to depend a lot on the weather.

Size isn't everything. Even the smallest circle has 360 degrees.

People who walk in another's tracks leave no prints.

Opportunity may knock, but it will never open the door on its own.

If it weren't for underachievers, no one could be above average.

A great pleasure in life is doing what others say you can't.

Life should be deeper than it is long.

When you can't change the direction of the wind, adjust your sails.

A #2 pencil and a dream can take you anywhere.

The art of life is knowing the right time to say things.

Not one shred of evidence supports the notion that life is serious.

Life may not be the party we had hoped for, but while we're here we might as well dance.

Belief is a truth held in the mind; faith is a fire in the heart.

The world is divided into people who do things and people who get the credit. Try to belong to the first class. There's far less competition.

Everything has beauty, but not everyone sees it.

One of the most complicated tasks modern mankind faces is trying to figure out how to lead a simple life.

We work so hard to keep the outside presentable when the inside is what really matters.

The trouble with reaching a crossroad in life is the lack of signposts.

Life is like a piano - what you get out of it depends on how you play it.

Get your soul in tune with God before the concert begins.

# Life

Peace of mind is not the absence of conflict from life, but the ability to cope with it.

You can't control the length of your life, but you can control the width and depth.

The purpose of existence is not to make a living, but to make a life.

Three things make us content: the seeing eye, the hearing ear, the responsive heart.

The thread that knits the movement into a living pattern is change.

It's not so important where we are standing, but in what direction we are moving.

We all can't be shining examples, but we can all twinkle a little.

Put a little more love in living, and you will love life more than ever before.

A task worth doing and friends worth having make life worthwhile.

What we must decide is how we are valuable - rather than how valuable we are.

Where we go hereafter depends on what we go after here.

Life is like an ever shifting kaleidoscope - a slight change and all patterns alter.

Only you can be yourself. No one else is qualified for the job.

Good words and good deeds
keep life's garden free of weeds.

Life is a measure to be filled and not a cup to empty.

Life is like an escalator - you can move forward or backward, you can not remain still.

It is a man that makes truth great,
not truth that makes man great.

What would life be if we had no courage to attempt?

The art of living lies in a fine mingling of letting go and holding on.

We must have a dream if we are going to make a dream come true.

Get as much chocolate out of life as you can.

One of the wonders of life is just that - the wonder of life.

The entire sum of existence is the magic of being needed by just one person.

There are no absolute answers to life - just revelations.

Some people are so busy being good they forget they should be busy doing good.

No person was ever honored for what he received; honor is the reward for what he gave.

Life is uncertain - eat dessert first.

The handsome gifts that fate and nature lends us, most often are the very ones that end us.

Life is like an onion - you peel it off one layer at a time, and sometimes it makes you weep.

Life is a flame that is always burning itself out, but it catches fire again every time a child is born.

Grief's best music is hope.

Far and away the best prize that life offers is the chance to work hard at work worth doing.

Every person's life is a fairy tale written by God's fingers.

Conceit may puff a man up, but never prop him up.

Character is that which reveals moral purpose, exposing the class of things a man chooses or avoids.

Hope is a wish that won't go away.

Life is a lot like a vacation – we are so fixed on the idea of where we're going that we don't appreciate where we are.

Those who get the most out of life are those who don't ask much from it.

# Life

Life is a game - and it comes without instructions.

May you live as long as you want, and never want as long as you live.

Solitary people are never alone.

The school of life is a compulsory education that no one escapes.

The only thing that one really knows about human nature is that it changes.

To truly live is the rarest thing in the world. Most people exist - that is all.

The perfection of man lies not in what a man has, but in what man is.

Life is a dance. Don't sit it out.

The secret of life is never to have an emotion that is unbecoming.

Life is never fair. And perhaps it is a good thing for most of us that it is not.

When one door is shut, another opens.

It's a funny thing about life; if you refuse to accept anything but the best, you very often get it.

Miracles happen to those who believe in them.

The ten most powerful two-letter words are "If it is to be, it is up to me."

The greatest thing in life is to be needed.

Change is inevitable, except from a vending machine.

Life is sexually transmitted.

Reality is, to a good extent, what we want it to be.

If you have accomplished all that you planned for your life, you have not planned enough.

Whatever your talent, use it in every way possible. Spend it lavishly like a millionaire intent on going broke.

One person with a dream is equal to ninety-nine who only have an interest.

Life is like a book - sometimes we must close one chapter and begin the next.

Life is not a spectacle or a feast; it is a predicament.

The secret of life isn't what happens to you, but what you do with what happens to you.

Footprints on the sands of time are not made by sitting down.

Life is a work of art, designed by the one who lives it.

Change is not really an optional thing.

The greatest battles of life are fought out daily in the silent chambers of the soul

The deepest hunger of the human heart is to be understood.

If you don't run your own life, somebody else will.

Life is like a box of hand grenades - you never know what will blow you to kingdom come.

Don't compromise yourself. You are all you have.

What is lovely never dies, but passes into loveliness.

We promise according to our hopes, and perform according to our fears.

To enjoy time alone, you must first appreciate the person you are with.

The only way to have a life is to commit to it like crazy.

You can't shoplift from life. We don't get away with anything we don't pay for.

Not what we gain, but what we give
measures the worth of the life we live.

It is not a tragedy to have only one talent. The tragedy is in not using it.

Life is like a decks of cards - we can't help the hand that is dealt us, but we can help the way we play it.

We need to make the most of life each day before it flies away.

# Life

Your living is determined not so much by what life brings to you, as by the attitude you bring to life.

The first step in anything new is having confidence in you.

There is only one corner of the universe you can be certain of improving, and that is your own self.

Life is like a ten-speed bike - we all have gears we never use.

Life's a real bumpy road. What you need to do is develop good shock absorbers.

The three F's: forgive, forget, and forge ahead.

Life is like a blind date - sometimes you just have to have a little faith.

Life is full of such sadness and sorrow, sometimes I think it's better not to be born at all, but how many people do you meet in a lifetime who were that lucky?

The greatest of faults is to be conscious of none.

The rule of my life is to make business my pleasure, and pleasure my business.

Life is like a taxi-the meter that keeps on ticking whether you're getting anywhere or not.

The most important thing in every day life is absolute honesty; once you learn to fake that, life is a cinch.

It's not how long the row that matters - it's how you pick the beans.

Life's most persistent and urgent question is, "What are you doing for others?"

A man's life is dyed the color of his imagination.

Our business in life is not to get ahead of others, but to get ahead of ourselves.

Your life might be the only bible some people ever read, so live accordingly.

Some people insist on going through life pushing all the doors marked 'pull'.

# Life

Life is too hard to trust no one.

The important thing about your lot in life is whether you use it for parking or for building.

Learning to live is learning to let go.

Life is like a sandwich - the more you add to it, the better it becomes.

In the midst of everything, take time to love and laugh and pray.
Then life will be worth living, each and every day.

Life is like a shower - one wrong turn and you end up in hot water.

Don't let life discourage you. Everyone who got where he is had to begin where he was.

Life is like a car - the slower you go, the longer you'll last.

Learn to be patient; a woman spends two-thirds of her life waiting for something or someone.

Sometimes in life, situations develop that only the half crazy can get out of.

It's bad enough to poke along, but it would be much worse
to travel the road of life with gears stuck in reverse.

If we want life to run smoothly, we must grease it with gratitude.

When life gives you lemons, make lemonade. When life gives you scraps, make quilts.

One of life's little surprises is receiving in the mail the rebate check you forgot about.

Put a little more into living, and you will love life more than ever before.

It is the simple things in life that make living worthwhile - love and duty, Work and rest, living close to nature.

Poor is the man who cannot enjoy the simple things of life.

Life is too short to remember slights and insults
to hold grudges that rob you of happiness
to waste time doing things that are of no value.

A pessimist is a person who is seasick during the entire voyage of life.

# Life

While traveling along the road of life, enjoy the going and stop thinking so fiercely about getting there.

Consideration for others is the basis of a good life.

Life is just one long vacation to people who love their work.

A pessimist is a person who takes life with a grain of salt.

Watch out for the little things in life; a fish bone is much more dangerous than a soup bone.

It takes only a moment to hug a child but a lifetime is often too short for him to forget it.

Potential has a short shelf life.

The man who is getting the most out of life has already made ample provision for the worst.

Good deeds are Certificates of Deposit invested in our future when the Book of Life is balanced.

Life often pulls the rug out from under people who always demand the red carpet treatment.

Too many of us expect life to serve the dessert before we've eaten our veggies.

The capacity of receiving pleasure from common things is one of the secrets of a happy life.

Think of life as a good book. The further you get into it, the more it begins to make sense.

If you have doubt about doing something, ask yourself if you would do it if it were the last hour of your life.

Life is a long lesson in humility.

Most men's life is often a contest between brains and glands.

The idea of life is to get a little more happiness than destiny planned to give us.

Nobody has a harder time going through life than the fellow who tries to take it soft.

Times are different. Now the facts of life are about the birds and the bees and the viruses.

The latter part of a wise man's life is taken up in curing all of the follies, prejudices, and false opinions he has contracted in the former part.

What folks say probably won't influence your life; how you respond undoubtedly will.

If you can dance with adversity, you'll never be out of step with life.

People who have no respect for other forms of life usually have little respect for their own lives.

Life is like an exciting book, and every day starts a new chapter.

The three immutable facts of life:
you will get stuff,
you will die, and
someone will get that stuff.

You cannot enjoy life without contributing to it.

A man who has work that suits him and a woman, whom he loves, has squared his accounts with life.

One of life's greatest crimes is theft of a child's trust.

What's the difference between school and life? In school, you're taught a lesson and then given a test. In life, you're given a test that teaches you a lesson.

Life is like a bridge - cross over it, but don't establish yourself upon it.

As long as you have a window, life is exciting.

In three words I can sum up everything I've learned about life. It goes on.

A life that touches the hearts of others goes on forever.

Life

# Bert's Observations

## **Observations**

It is good for my ego that, at my age and state of decrepitude, my opinions are still considered of value.

I may have my faults, but being wrong isn't one of them.

Junk is stuff we throw away.
Stuff is junk we keep.

If you want the world to be at a path to your door, just try to take a nap on a Saturday afternoon.

Car phones are great, when you're going down hill on the freeway with a huge tractor-trailer on our bumper, you can dial a prayer.

Remember - every shut-eye isn't asleep!

Give a man a fish and you feed him for a day. Teach him to fish and you get rid of him on weekends.

A soft answer turneth away wrath, but not telephone sales people.

Fewer accidents are caused by traffic jams than by pickled drivers.

Just because you have the right to do something, doesn't make it the right thing to do.

Why is it that if we work four days, they call it a 'short work week', but if we relax for three days, they call it a 'long weekend'?

The trouble with wishful thinking is that it is usually ninety-nine percent wishful and one percent thinking.

Do you want to have breakfast with me? Should I call you or nudge you?

Used-car dealer, driving up a hill, "This is the opportunity of your lifetime."
Customer, "Yes, I can hear it knocking."

Why didn't the skeleton go to the dance?
He had no body to go with.

There's nothing wrong with wanting to change the world, but first start with yourself.

# Bert's Observations

Horse owner, "I told you to rush around that last turn! Why didn't you follow orders?
Jockey, "Because it didn't seem fair to leave the horse behind."

There is a very fine line between 'hobby' and 'mental illness'.

I can fix anything. Where's the duct tape?

If you watch a game, it's fun.
If you play it, it's recreation.
If you work at it, it's golf.

May all your troubles last as long as your new year's resolutions.

The expert magician seeks to deceive the mind, rather than the eye.

If the shoe fits, you're not allowing for growth.

What do sea monsters eat?
Fish and ships.

Human beings are optimists. They believe they have a good chance to win a lottery, but not the slightest chance of getting injured in a traffic accident.

A guilty conscience is God's woodshed.

Narrow minds and wide mouths go together.

A perfectionist is a person who takes infinite pains and gives them to others.

I am not perfect, but so close it scares me.

Sin has many tools, but a lie is the handle which fits them all.

The task before us is never greater than the power behind us.

Adapt or perish now as ever, is nature's inexorable imperative.

Conscience is the inner voice which warns us that someone may be looking.

If pleasures are greatest in anticipation, just remember this is also true of trouble.

Patience is blending moral courage with physical timidity.

## Bert's Observations

In skating over thin ice, safety is in our speed.

There is no one so bound to his own face that he doesn't cherish the hope of presenting another to the world.

Don't look a gift-horse in the mouth.

What are we if we don't try?

Nothing is ever as easy as it looks.

A ship is safe in the harbor, but that isn't what ships were built for.

The trouble with some people is that they would rather pray for forgiveness than fight temptation.

Never meet trouble halfway. It is quite capable of making the entire journey alone.

What goes around, comes around.

Discretion is the better part of valor.

Those who cannot dance say the music is no good.

Those who are fond of setting things to rights have no great objection to seeing them wrong.

Some people are like buttons, always popping off.

Don't worry, be crabby.

A vacationer caught a fish so big he dislocated both his shoulders describing it.

Vacations would be a lot more pleasant if you could stop the lawn along with the newspaper and the mail.

Nature creates wonders that science only contemplates.

Better to be square than to move in the wrong circles.

Honesty once pawned is never redeemed.

Most of our worries are re-runs.

Wrinkled with care and worry? Get your faith lifted.

Many of us are more capable than some of us, but none of us is as capable as all of us.

If the world is cold, make it your business to build fires.

Without courage, all other virtues lose their meaning.

The shortest distance between two points is often under construction.

You can always tell an egotist, but you can't tell him much.

Be careful not to dull your conscience through neglect; it may never speak to you again.

The drum knows its owner's hands.

Junk is the thing you keep for ten years and the sell in a garage sale two days before you need it.

A windshield scraper is a plastic gadget that falls out of your glove box all summer, hides under the seat all winter, then breaks when you want to use it.

You can either agree with me or be wrong.

Drive-in banks give cars a chance to see what their real owners look like.

Ever wonder how the size of hail was described before the game of golf was invented?

Travelers can tell when it's vacation time - the roads are closed and the detours are open.

Some people are so indecisive, their favorite color is plaid.

The two greatest hazards on the road today are people over 65 driving under 25 and those under 25 driving over 65.

Worrying is like sitting in a rocking chair. It gives you something to do, but it doesn't get you anywhere.

The average tourist wants to go to places where there are no tourists.

We keep making highways wider so more cars can get in the same accident.

If you want to get even with someone in the worst way, you probably will.

## Bert's Observations

Ever notice how people say everything happens for the best, but it's always said when something bad happens.

People who say, 'Anything is possible', have never tried to complain to a recorded announcement.

The truly free man is the one who will turn down an invitation to dinner without giving an excuse.

The surest way to get an honest answer is to put the question to a six-year old.

There really is no witness so terrible, no accuser so powerful as the conscience that dwells in each of us.

Why is it that the last place you saw something that you are looking for is almost never where it is now?

What's stranger than seeing a catfish?
Seeing a goldfish bowl.

Why is it that when you only have one item and there's no one ahead of you in the checkout line, the cashier decides to change the register tape?

When I'm right, no one remembers. When I'm wrong, no one forgets.

Normally, they couldn't pay me enough to get on an airplane, so I find out which ones are overbooked and let them pay me to get off.

I was gratified to be able to answer promptly, and I did. I said I didn't know.

I can't complain, but sometimes, I still do.

Thanks to TV we get more bad news in an hour than we used to get in a week.

If I have to wait twenty-four hours to report my wife missing, what am I supposed to do for dinner tonight?

It's amazing how there are people who say, "The Lord is my shepherd" and then try and outfox Him.

A well-adjusted person is one who makes the same mistake twice without getting nervous.

It's not the action, it's the intention behind the action.

# Bert's Observations

What passes for confidence is often vanity.

When the label reads 'maintenance free', it usually means that when it breaks it can't be fixed.

Tossing out items you haven't used for years is like trimming your fingernails - three hours later you need them.

Whoever said getting there is half the fun never had to get to the airport during rush hour

Plastic is responsible for strong language about weak forks.

How do you get down from an elephant?
You don't, you get down from a goose.

If we couldn't take it with us, there would be a lot more towels in hotel rooms.

What did the cannibal order on his pizza?
Everybody.

If all the cars in the world were laid end to end on a US highway, some fool would still try to pass.

Early to bed and early to rise makes a man wish he didn't have to go to work.

The only thing worse than being alone is wishing you were.

Faith is the key to fit the door of hope, but there is no power like love for turning it.

Don't let anyone tell you that you're worthless, you can always be used as a bad example.

Work is for people who don't know how to play golf.

A foot is the best device for finding furniture in the dark.

Why can't they build planes out of the same indestructible material that their little black boxes are made of?

Give a man a fish, and you have fed him for a day. Teach a man to fish, and he'll keep worms in the fridge.

## Bert's Observations

Why is it that the people seated behind you in a movie theater never talk during a really bad movie?

If at first you don't succeed, you'll get a lot of advice from other folks who didn't succeed either.

The worst driver in the world is always a jump ahead of you.

Alexander Graham Bell quit while he was ahead. He invented the telephone - he didn't invent the busy signal.

Who-so-ever tooteth not his horn, the same shall not be tooted.

The man who says, "Stop me if I'm wrong," usually thinks he isn't.

People will believe anything if you whisper it.

The early bird has to get his own breakfast.

Everyone has the right to some faults, but there are those who abuse the privilege.

The only ones whose troubles are behind them are school bus drivers.

An expert is someone who is called in at the last minute to share the blame.

Short shoes and long corns to my enemies!

Don't tell me that worrying doesn't do any good. I know better. The things I worry about don't happen.

Why are women wearing perfumes that smell like flowers to attract men? Men don't like flowers. They should wear a scent called new car interior.

They say that animal behavior can warn you when an earthquake is coming. The night before the last earthquake hit, our family dog took the car keys and drove to Arizona.

What a hotel! The towels were so fluffy I could hardly close my suitcase.

The closest we ever come to perfection is when we write our resumes.

Dishonesty is like a boomerang. About the time you think all is well, it hits you in the back of the head.

# Bert's Observations

I bought a car at a police auction. When I got it home, I found a dead body handcuffed in the trunk. Actually it isn't that bad, now I can use the car pool lane.

I'll be sober tomorrow, but you'll be crazy the rest of your life.

I know God won't give me more than I can handle. I just wish He didn't trust me so much.

If the shoe fits buy it in every color.

Going to church doesn't make you a Christian any more than standing in a garage makes you a mechanic.

Don't forget, Lady Godiva put everything she had on a horse.

If at first you don't succeed, try, try again. Then quit. No use being a damn fool about it.

I was in love with a beautiful blonde once. She drove me to drink. It is the one thing I'm indebted to her for.

The nice thing about air travel is that you're usually too scared to be bored.

Pro football is like nuclear warfare, there are no winners, only survivors.

Why do people object to nudity? It's only skin.

Unsafe cars are recalled by the maker, this happens to unsafe drivers too.

The mind of the bigot is like the pupil of the eye; the more light you pour up on it, the more it will contract.

One thing about being an armchair athlete - when you go from football to basketball, you don't have to change your uniform.

Some people cause happiness wherever they go,
some cause happiness whenever they go.

A man convinced against his will
is of the same opinion still.

If you are not part of the solution, you are part of the problem.

The know-it-all knows what to do until it happens to him.

## Bert's Observations

The right to do something does not mean that doing it is right.

Remember when people who did windows included gas station attendants?

When playing golf, if you can't be good, at least be quick.

Some people have eyes that see not and ears that hear not, but never tongues that talk not.

The great trouble with an idle rumor is, it doesn't remain so.

He who sows thorns should never go barefoot.

You can speak to the point without being sharp.

We should never get caught in our own mouthtrap.

Maybe people should swap problems. Everyone knows how to solve the other guy's.

Nothing is ever really lost; it's just where it doesn't belong.

Blessed are the flexible, for they shall not be bent out of shape.

God gives us the ingredients for our daily bread, but He expects us to do the baking.

Some people treat their religion like a spare tire, they never expect to use it, except in an emergency.

Only God is in a position to look down on everyone.

You'll never get the busy signal on the prayer line to heaven.

When you meet temptation, turn to the right.

The main difficulty with lying is the necessity of having a good memory.

One who thinks by the inch and moves by the yard needs to be moved by the foot.

Whoever fights monsters should see to it that, in the process he does not become a monster.

If it wasn't for bad luck I wouldn't have any luck at all.

# Bert's Observations

Living it up is a quick way to build a reputation that you may be long in trying to live down.

Musicians don't retire; they stop when there's no more music in them.

When the flasher walked up to a little old lady and opened up his rain coat. She studied him a moment and said, "You call that a lining?"

The internet is an audience of one, a billion times over.

I can see through my bifocals;
my dentures fit me fine;
my hearing aid does wonders,
but Lord, I miss my mind.

I first began to like girls the minute I discovered they weren't boys.

My wife wanted a foreign convertible - I got her one, a rickshaw.

I find television very educating. Every time somebody turns on the set I go into the other room and read a book.

It's easy to tune out your critics, but difficult to turn off your conscience.

Assume a virtue, if you have it or not.

It takes a lot of courage to show your dreams to someone else.

Money won't create success, the freedom to make it will.

It is in your moments of decision that your destiny is shaped.

Nothing can stop the man with the right mental attitude from achieving his goal and nothing on earth can help the man with the wrong mental attitude.

No noise is as emphatic as one you are trying not to listen to.

If you can't be kind, at least be vague.

God doesn't have to put His name on a sign in the corner of a meadow, because nobody else makes meadows.

The trouble with speaking one's mind is that it limits conversations.

The tongue - we spend three years learning how to use it and the rest of our lives learning how to control it.

## Bert's Observations

There is no pleasure in having nothing to do; the fun is having lots to do and not doing it.

Take the word 'indolence', it makes laziness seem classy.

Nothing is opened more often by mistake than the mouth.

God wisely designed the human body so that we can neither pat our own backs nor kick ourselves too easily.

Anticipating is even more fun than recollecting.

It's not whether you win or lose, but how you place the blame.

The way some people find fault, you'd think there was a reward.

Those who think they know it all are very annoying to those who do.

The only thing wrong with doing nothing is that you never know when you're finished.

If at first you don't succeed - find someone who knows what he's doing.

One is tolerant only of that which does not concern him.

One good thing about talking to yourself is that you always have a rapt audience.

There are two periods when fishing is good, before you get there and after you leave.

Young priests listening to confessions must learn to refrain from saying "Wow!"

There is always an easy solution to every problem - neat, plausible, or wrong.

With jeans there's no problem finding the right size - one size hurts all.

Fresh flowers are acceptable. Fresh mouths are not.

In this world it rains on the Just and the Unjust alike, but the Unjust have the Just's umbrellas.

It is better to be a coward for a minute than dead for the rest of your life.

Today it isn't facing the music that hurts, it's listening to it.

An important part of praying is a willingness to become part of the answer.

It's not good enough that we do our best; sometimes we have to do what is required.

What crops up may not be what we wish we had planted.

Last year I made a list of things to do.
I'll use that list again this year,
It's still as good as new.

Burn the candles at both ends and you double the chances of getting your fingers burned.

One thing I've learned in growing old,
no doubt you've noticed too:
The kids to whom you gave advice
now give advice to you.

The trouble with the younger generation is that it hasn't read the minutes of the last meeting.

Seeing ourselves as others see us wouldn't do any good. We wouldn't believe it.

If water pollution gets any worse, walking on it will be a cinch.

Why are the godless everywhere so frightened by the sound of prayer?

I have always been in the right place at the right time. Of course, I steered myself there.

If at first you don't succeed, try looking in the wastebasket.

For every credibility gap there is a gullibility fill.

Just about the time a man gets his temper under control, he goes out and plays golf again.

The easiest thing to decide is what you would do if you were in someone else's shoes.

There was a time when the only way you got hot lunch at school was to leave it near the radiator.

Put everything in God's hand and eventually you will see God's hand in everything.

## Bert's Observations

Irony is when you buy a suit with two pairs of pants, and then burn a hole in the jacket

Television will never replace the newspaper. You can't swat a fly with a rolled-up TV.

Most people are willing to change, not because they see the light, but because they feel the heat.

If everything is coming your way, you're in the wrong lane.

Some people are only stubborn when they don't get their way.

The only sharp-edged tool that gets sharper with use is the tongue.

A pickle is a cucumber soured by a jarring experience.

In the old days, when a young man started sowing his wild oats, his father started the thrashing machine.

Live your life so you wouldn't be afraid to sell your parrot to the town gossip.

To err is human, but to think of someone to blame it on is genius.

All generalizations are dangerous - even this one.

All the best coaches are in the stands.

Always be sincere, even if you don't mean it.

The easiest way to sleep is to count your blessings instead of your problems.

An optimist sees the glass as half full,
a pessimist sees it as half empty, and
a realist sees it as one more thing to wash.

Hindsight tells us that Adam's rib was the original bone of contention.

The trouble with many people who stop to count their blessings is their arithmetic is so poor.

Advertisement for lawn sprinkler system: "Dew it yourself."

When it comes to blame, more people than cars are equipped with automatic shifts.

# Bert's Observations

Ambition can change the appealing into the appalling.

Forgiveness is often easier once you realize that you have no one to blame but yourself.

A true test of patience is not minding being put on hold.

Other's faults are like the headlights of an oncoming car; they seem more glaring than our own.

Just because the river is quiet, doesn't mean the crocodiles have left.

I've never had a problem that was as easy to solve as someone else's.

You can't get rid of a bad temper by losing it.

When you see how slow some people are, you wonder how they can call us the human race.

A key chain enables you to do such stunts as losing all your keys at once.

Everyone is a moon, and has a dark side which he never shows to anybody.

Whether you think health or wealth is more important depends upon which one you have lost.

You are a good man if you can suppress even a little glee at an enemy's problem.

People like attention. There aren't many things we will continue to do if nobody notices.

The real reason mountain climbers tie themselves together is to keep the sensible ones from going home.

Sauna sign: "out of order - no sweat."

Why is it when you dial the wrong number it is never busy?

Strong men can always afford to be gentle. Only the weak are intent on "giving as they get."

The subject of deepest interest to an average human is himself.

Never fly with an airline who's "Welcome Aboard" spiel begins with, "Be the good Lord willing. . ."

## Bert's Observations

The only perfect mates come in shoes and gloves.

Nothing cooks a person's goose quicker than a hot temper.

Why is sex so popular?
It has no calories.

If you have reached a dead end, it could be that you're sitting on it.

The sure way to make a lost object turn up: Buy a replacement.

No person was ever honored for what he received. Honor is the reward for what he gave.

I am half way between retired and retarded.

It is when all play safe that we create a world of utmost insecurity.

When you finally go back to your old hometown, you find it wasn't the old home you missed, but your childhood.

You know a movie is bad when they show it on an airplane and people walk out.

The deepest principle of human nature is the craving to he appreciated.

We tend to believe whatever is told to us in strict confidence.

If we are all in the same boat, why is it that only some of us are doing all the rowing?

I am not against sex. I am here as a result of sex.

Most of our problems are caused by easy solutions to other's problems.

A picnic is when you take what you have in the house, put it between slices of bread, drive to some distant spot, and share it with the ants.

You can't believe anything you hear these days, but you can repeat it.

In religion as in friendship, they who profess most are the least sincere.

Our society is more preoccupied with ingesting dietary fiber than with instilling moral fiber.

For most of us, a moral issue is on right, wrong, and everybody does it.

# Bert's Observations

When we say that something happened by chance, what we really mean is that we haven't discovered what caused it.

Serenity is achieved by resolutely facing life's problems and finally realizing that for many of them, nothing can be done.

If you are lucky enough to be Irish, you are lucky enough.

The unforgivable crime is soft hitting. Do not hit at all if it can be avoided, but never hit softly.

Honor is like the eye, which cannot suffer the least impurity without damage. It is a precious stone, the price of which is lessened by a single flaw.

Good manners could prevent more accidents than improved highways.

The most underdeveloped territory on earth is situated between human ears.

If you are green with envy, you are ripe for trouble.

Everybody thinks of changing humanity and nobody thinks of changing himself.

Bores are folks who know only one subject - or those who know something about every subject.

Science may have found a cure for most evils, but it has found no remedy for the worst of them all - apathy.

Better be square than to move in the wrong circles.

What did they give to the man who invented the door knocker?
The No-bell prize.

To be nobly wrong is more manly than to be meanly right.

Ten two-letter words worth remembering: IF IT IS TO BE, IT IS UP TO ME.

Arguments are the worst sort of conversation.

The grouch who thinks the world is against him, may he right.

Conscience usually doesn't come out of the closet until someone opens the door.

# Bert's Observations

You really are lucky! Just imagine if your errors were published every day like those of a ballplayer.

Driving as if you are on your way to the dentist's is a good, safe speed.

What kind of nut sits on a wall?
A walnut.

It's the other driver you have to watch out for, he may he stupid too.

A man who finds no satisfaction in himself seeks for it in vain elsewhere.

Lots of lives are ruined because so many incompetent drivers drive and so many unqualified advisers advise.

In still waters are the largest fish.

Stay in touch; absence makes the heart grow wonder.

Its strange how sincerely a man says, "I guess I failed to make myself clear," it sounds like he is saying, "You idiot how can I make you understand?"

Temptation can defeat reputation if the stakes are high enough.

A small town is a place where you recognize the inventory at a garage sale.

"How are you," is a greeting, not a question.

I'm not bossy, I just have better ideas.

Angels can fly, because they take themselves lightly.

It doesn't pay to worry, and if it did, I'd probably be overqualified for the job.

One disadvantage with having nothing to do is you can't stop and rest.

The most effective water power in the world is tears.

A new broom sweeps clean, but the old broom knows the corners.

There should be a better reward for promptness than having to wait for everyone else.

All charming people are spoiled. It is the secret of their attraction.

# Bert's Observations

A conservative is a man who is too cowardly to fight and too fat to run.

I can resist anything but temptation; my will is strong, but my won't is weak.

Even a small thorn causes pain.

Warning: People who have an attitude know how to use it.

We'll never know what an average person thinks until we can find one who will admit he's average.

It is the quiet pigs that eat the meal.

Tears do not always mean a person is sad.

I can only please one person per day. Today is not your day. Tomorrow doesn't look good either.

May leprechauns strew happiness wherever you walk each day and Irish angels smile on you all along the way.

Bad is never good, until worse happens.

If I only had a little humility, I would be perfect.

While an original is always hard to find, he is easy to recognize.

There is no pleasure in having nothing to do; the fun is in having lots to do and not doing it.

If you would sleep soundly; take a clear conscience to bed.

Walking isn't a lost art - one must, by some means, get to the car.

A thousand mile trip begins with a short walk - the one you take to go back to see if you turned off the lights.

The best way to win an argument is to begin by being right.

May all your troubles last as long as your New Year's resolutions.

Nothing is impossible for the man who doesn't have to do it himself.

When I am alone in my room, I have a beautiful singing voice.

# Bert's Observations

It's embarrassing to have a glamour photograph made of yourself and not have anyone recognize that it's you.

It's no fun putting on a wet swimsuit.

You always know the right thing to do. The hard part is doing it.

It's not a good idea to put bubble bath in a Jacuzzi.

You can tell a lot about a person by looking in the trunk of his car.

It's not a good idea to try to break in a new bra during a transcontinental flight.

Even with the lights out, I can still find the cashews in the mixed nuts.

The sole cause of man's unhappiness is that he does not know how to stay quietly in his room.

Blessed are the hard-of-hearing, for they miss much small talk.

Truth doesn't hurt unless it ought to.

If you cannot make light of your troubles, keep them in the dark.

Worry is like a rocking chair; it will give you some thing to do, but it won't get you anywhere.

Heaven has no rage like love to hatred turned, nor hell a fury like a woman scorned.

Assassination is the sincerest form of flattery.

Lead me not into temptation, for I shall find it myself.

No matter how clear the river, there is always some darkness upstream drifting down toward you.

Good voices do not always belong to good faces.

You paint a mouse into a corner and a tiger comes out.

Irish proverb - forgive your enemies, but get even first.

Real men don't waste their hormones growing hair.

I used up all my sick days, so I called in dead.

# Bert's Observations

Upon the advice of my attorney, my shirt bears no message at this time.

If you remember the 60's, you weren't really there.

Water vapor gets together in a cloud. When it is big enough to be called a drop, it does.

Mushrooms always grow in damp places, which is why they look like umbrellas.

The word 'trousers' is an uncommon noun, because it is singular at the top and plural at the bottom.

Revenge is a dish best eaten cold.

When planets run around and around in circles, we say they are orbiting. When people do it, we say they are crazy.

Children inhabitants of Moscow are called mosquitoes.

The spinal column is a long bunch of bones, the head sits on the top, and you sit on the bottom.

Rehab is for quitters.

Some day, we may discover how to make magnets that can point in any direction.

A vibration is a motion that cannot make up its mind which way it wants to go.

My designated driver drove me to drink.

I yell because I care.

Two wrongs don't make a right, but two Wrights made an airplane.

The problem with the gene pool is that there is no lifeguard.

It's hard to make a comeback when you haven't been anywhere.

The only time the world beats a path to your door is if you're in the bathtub.

Never knock on death's door; ring the doorbell and run (the devil hates that).

# Bert's Observations

Vital papers will demonstrate their vitality by moving from where you left them to where you can't find them.

How can a slim chance and a fat chance be the same, while a wise man and a wise guy are opposites?

Why do noses run and feet smell?

Frankly, scallop, I don't give a clam.

I'm not suddenly a dirty old man. I've been practicing since 1941.

He who laughs last, thinks slowest.

Depression is merely anger without enthusiasm.

Support bacteria - they're the only culture some people have.

If at first you don't succeed, destroy all the evidence that you tried.

Never do card tricks for the group you play poker with.

Some people are only alive because murder is illegal.

We are born naked, wet, and hungry. Then things get worse.

There was an old man of Nan Tucket
who kept all his cash in a bucket,
but his daughter, named Nan,
ran away with a man,
and as for the bucket, Nan Tucket.

A mugwump is a fellow with his mug on one side of the fence, and his wump on the other.

A little nonsense now and then is relished by the best of men.

The optimist proclaims that we live in the best of all possible worlds; and the pessimist fears this is true.

Make it idiot-proof and someone will make a better idiot.

Ever stop to think and forget to start again?

A clear conscience is usually the sign of a bad memory.

Get a new car for your spouse. It will be a great trade.

A conclusion is the place where you got tired of thinking.

I love Thanksgiving, almost everyone seems to be in the spirit. Just today another driver called me a turkey and I told him to stuff it.

Non-fiction best seller: "How to avoid arguments" by Xavier Breth.

Sometimes it's very frightening to look back on our lives, because we realize how many of our mistakes were actually carefully planned out.

There's little 'original sin' left anymore; everything has been tried before.

The irony of the information age is that it has given new respectability to uniformed opinion.

It's not premarital sex if you don't plan on getting married.

If aliens are smart enough to travel through space, why do they keep abducting the dumbest people on earth?

Don't argue for a later bed time while you're wearing pajamas with feet.

Picking your nose when no one is looking is still picking your nose.

Hiding peas under your napkin only works once.

You only go down the slide head first one time.

Don't say, "The last one there is a rotten egg," unless you're absolutely sure there's a slow kid behind you.

You will have much more respect for a bird after you try making a nest.

Homesick is the worst kind of sick.

Courage is not the absence of fear, but the concealing of it.

Civilization is simply an organization that man has developed in order that he may live in peace with his neighbors.

When cheese gets its picture taken, what does it say?

Do Lipton tea employees take coffee breaks?

You never really learn to swear until you learn to drive.

## Bert's Observations

If a person with multiple personalities threatens suicide, is that considered a hostage situation.

The end of all our exploring will be to arrive where we started and know the place for the first time.

There is no pillow as soft as a clear conscience.

Faith is absurd, and so is love. You have to trust.

There are three kinds of untruths, lies, damn lies, and statistics.

No one can make a fool out of you without your permission.

'If only' are wretched words.

After all, what is a lie? Tis but the truth in masquerade.

In my day, we ate indoors and went to the toilet outdoors. Now we eat outdoors and go to the toilet indoors.

Deal with honor and sleep at night.

The bad scorn the good and the crooked despise the straight.

Crime to many is not a crime, but simply a way of life.

A private prayer: May I deal with honor, may I act with courage, and may I achieve humility.

True patience means waiting without worrying.

Your village called - their idiot is missing.

Beware of all enterprises that require new clothes.

If it's going to be two against one, make sure you're not the one.

Why buy roses when daisies are free.

Remember who gives wet kisses, and the next time you see them, wave from across the room.

Nobody notices it when your zipper is up, but everyone notices when it's down.

You won't find average Americans on the left or the right. You will find them at K-Mart.

I need to have the means to take care of myself for the next few years. Therapy is not cheap.

I feel a little bit like Elizabeth Taylor's eighth husband, I know what to do, but I have to find a new and more interesting way to do it.

People feel so enslaved by technology that they will stop having sex to answer the telephone.

Some times I think I'm known for something that's not so great to be known for.

I know a guy who considers himself a real Romeo. He makes Bill Clinton look like Mary Poppins.

People who live in glass houses don't have much of a sex life.

It's good to be alone without being lonely.

Confusion is a term we have invented to describe an order of things that is not yet understood.

Hope is the feeling you have that the feeling you have is not permanent.

I base most of my fashion taste on what doesn't itch.

When man learned that he could not live by bread alone, he invented the sandwich.

If the shoe fits, get another one just like it.

I don't have all the answers, just the ones that matter.

Sex is a misdemeanor - The more I miss, de meaner I get.

Do you think you can be alone in this world and not be lonely?

If at first you don't succeed, skydiving is not for you.

Too bad stupidity isn't painful.

The beatings will continue until morale improves.

Pregnancy is not a communicable disease.

## Bert's Observations

Most men's lives are often a contest between brains and glands.

Being a survivor has to mean more than just staying alive.

Have a long spoon when you eat with the devil.

Buy a used car with the same caution a naked man uses to climb a barbed wire fence.

Anyone can cook a trout. The real art is in hooking the darned thing.

I'm only a vegetarian when I am personally acquainted with the animal in question.

Hot is hot only when you have cold to compare it with.

People do not see the world as it is; they see it as they are, or as they have been conditioned to be.

Resentment hurts only those who harbor it.

You can go anywhere you want if you look serious and carry a clipboard.

When you don't know what to do, walk fast and look worried.

How much deeper would oceans be if sponges didn't live there?

If it's true that we are here to help others, then what exactly are the others here for?

No one ever says, "It's only a game," when their team is winning.

Sex is a Braille experience.

If you take an oriental person and spin him around several times, does he become disoriented?

Do you know someone whose reach exceeds his grasp?

Some men see things as they are, and say, why? I dream things that never were and say, why not?

The coroner's motto, "People are dying to meet us."

Some days, you're the dog; some days you're the hydrant.

The telephone is the underlying cause of modern man's inhumanity to man.

First you lie, then you swear to it, and then you make the sale.

Character builds slowly, but it can be torn down with incredible swiftness.

On this shrunken globe, men can no longer live as strangers.

Beauty is its own excuse.

I do not regret the things I have done, but those I did not do.

Trying to be right all the time is a very subtle way of being wrong.

Man invented language to satisfy his deep need to complain.

Lord, keep your arm around my shoulder and your hand over my mouth.

Reputation is character minus what you've been caught doing.

The secret of being a bore is to tell everything.

The person who is wrapped up in himself is generally overdressed.

Revenge is a kind of wild justice.

She was so thin, her face seemed to have been carved on insufficient stock.

The word accident was invented by weak people to excuse their mistakes.

A positive attitude is a powerful force.

Work is for people who don't fish.

Ten measures of speech descended on the world; women took nine and men one.

I can resist everything except temptation.

A truth that's told with bad intent
beats all the lies you can invent.

A day of worry is more exhausting than a week of work.

Criticism, I believe, is much more blessed to give than receive.

A good marriage would be between a blind wife and a deaf husband.

# Bert's Observations

The only way to perpetuate a lie is with more lies.

A woman's place is in the home, and she should go there right after work.

The trouble with flying into a rage is that the visibility is so poor.

Of course my mechanic is good. If he wasn't, would I keep going hack to him every week?

The world is not any worse than it was a hundred years ago. It's just that the satellites give us better coverage.

Which travels faster, heat or cold?
Heat, because you can catch cold.

No matter how many right things you do, you will be remembered for the wrong ones you did.

Two of the most dangerous things in America are guns and credit cards.

Pleasure is a sin, and sometimes sin is a pleasure.

If you're not kissing or sleeping, keep your eyes open.

Sign on bank president's desk: "In this bank, NO is a complete sentence."

Opera in English makes as much sense as baseball in Italian.

He wants to be cremated, because he doesn't believe in death.

If you have not asked "Why?" when things go good, you have no right to ask "Why?" when things go bad.

Never burn your bridges - you would be surprised how many times you may have to cross the same river.

I despise the pleasure of pleasing people whom I despise.

You should never cry over any thing that can't cry back.

If you hang something in a closet for a while it shrinks two sizes.

When I travel I always like a nice hotel suite where I can put up with my wife.

I do not want to belong to the kind of club that accepts people like me as a member.

# Bert's Observations

To save time, let's just assume I know everything.

The job of journalists is to comfort the afflicted and afflict the comfortable.

If you are going around in circles, maybe you are cutting corners.

Speak softly and carry a big stick; you will go far.

We have just enough religion to make us hate, but not enough to make us love one another.

The more things a man is ashamed of, the more respectable he is.

The worst thing about him is that when he isn't drunk, he's sober.

No one knows the weight of another's burdens.

Columbus should be admired not only for discovering America, but for having gone to search for it on the faith of an opinion.

Early gardens are planted on a pray-as-you-sow plan.

Scary movies are produced in Hollyweird.

When all else fails, read the instructions.

Burdens should never get us down, except on our knees to pray.

A small town is a place where the traffic doesn't have to be re-routed for the Fourth of July parade.

The two most important senses we have are horse and common.

You can't make many mistakes with your mouth shut.

God's best gift to us is not things, but opportunities.

A night watchman is a man who earns his living without doing a day's work.

One thorn of experience is worth a whole wilderness of warning.

Answers that sound good aren't necessarily good sound answers.

One thing about resisting temptation, you can be sure it will give you another chance.

## Bert's Observations

There must be a nerve that runs directly from the hands to the nose. As soon as you get both hands full, your nose starts to itch.

Promises are like snowballs - easy to make but hard to keep.

Religious experience is meant to be bread for daily use, not cake for special occasions.

A wreath in your window and goodwill in your heart make a very merry Christmas.

Blondes tease - redheads please.

One of the more delectable fruits of gardening comes in conversational harvest.

The recipe for success is one part skill, ninety-nine parts organization, and a dash of luck.

I once had a broad mind and a narrow waist, now it's the other way around.

When people say they 'won't be a minute', they are usually right.

Some folks have no more conscience than a cow in a stampede.

He, who forgives, ends the quarrel.

Those who won't mind their own business, soon have no business to mind.

The reason volunteers aren't paid is not because they're worthless, but because they're priceless.

I don't have an attitude problem. You have a perception problem.

Accept that some days you are the pigeon, and some days you are the statue.

To belittle is to be little.

The fastest way to find something you've misplaced is to buy a replacement for it.

A good memory is important, but the ability to forget, priceless.

It seems that more and more people are getting into religion because of profits rather than the prophets.

The manner in which it is given is worth more than the gift.

Notice in a church bulletin: "In memory of my wife, I am donating a loudspeaker to the church."

Some people change their ways when they see the light; others only when they feel the heat.

It is said single women enjoy fiction more than married women because most wives hear too much of it.

The measure of a man is not how tall he is, but how much his neighbors respect him.

Joy shared is joy doubled.
Sorrow shared is sorrow halved.

When I was a kid I didn't have money to go to a barber. Now that I have money I don't have the hair.

You can read some people like a book, but you can't shut them up as easily.

The American, by nature, is optimistic. He is experimental, an inventor, and a builder who builds best when called upon to build greatly.

Good character, like good soup, is usually homemade.

Nobody knows about your integrity, sincerity, talent, or your goodwill unless you give out some samples.

The sun is always shining somewhere.

I know not what the future holds, but I know who holds the future.

And that's the world in a nutshell - an appropriate receptacle.

Bert's Observations

# *Love*

## **Love**

Give the gift of love, it's returnable.

Fear is useless, faith is necessary, love is everything.

Love and time are the only two things that cannot be bought, but only spent.

Life is too short for resentment, not nearly long enough for love.

Love is always an appropriate gift.

Teach your hands to help and your heart to love.

Love those who add to your life, and love those who subtract from it. Each has taught you something - the former show you how to live, the latter, how not to.

The heart that loves is always young.

We never know how much we need to be loved until we are.

The morning of life consists simply of loving truly, and being truly loved.

The love you invest in others is like the rays of the sun hitting a polished mirror - its warmth will be reflected back to you throughout a lifetime.

Hold those you love with open hands.

You maintain a house with paint and plaster.
You maintain a home with love.

Nature has never betrayed her lovers.

Love is a disease that begins with a fever and ends with a pain.

Do you believe in love at first sight, or should I walk by you again?

We pardon as long as we love.

The worst thing in life to be without is love, but toilet paper comes in a close second.

The heart has its reasons, which reason does not understand.

When there is love in the home, there is joy in the heart.

The fate of love is that it always seems too little or too much.

Faults are thick where love is thin.

What's stitched with love will never tear.

Love is the only game at which two can play and both can win.

The heart holds things the mind forgets.

Show me a guy who left his heart In San Francisco and I'll show you a guy with a hole in his chest.

Love enriches; it doesn't rehabilitate.

To love oneself is the beginning of a lifelong romance.

Some things are loved because they are valuable; others are valuable because they are loved.

Tears are God's way of melting a heart that is frozen with grief.

The riches that are in the heart can never be stolen.

You can try to teach people what love is by loving them, but they will never know what love is until they love someone.

People bemoan the fact that love doesn't last; neither does an ice cream cone, but it's delicious while it does.

If your heart is full of love, you always have something to give.

You may give without loving, but you can't love without giving.

Some think it's holding on that makes us strong, sometimes it's letting go.

It is better to have loved and lost - provided no alimony is involved.

Imagine how much faster it would be for us to learn how to love if we began with a shared definition.

When someone you love becomes a memory, the memory becomes a treasure.

Life without love is like a tree without blossom and fruit.

Love

If you can't love people, find something about them to like, when they like you for it, you will love them.

The national pastime in Tahiti Is making love - us silly fools, we picked baseball.

Love can be like taking a picture – you are not sure how it will turn out.

Your feet will bring you to where your heart is.

The best wine makes the sharpest vinegar, so can the deepest love turn to the deadliest hate.

He who falls in love with himself will have no rivals.

No disguise can long conceal love where it exists, or long feign it where it is lacking.

When you're with someone who's supportive and adores you, it can't help but make you feel and look younger.

Love unspoken is a letter written, but not mailed.

Romance lives by repetition, and repetition converts an appetite into an art.

One should always be in love, which is the reason one should never marry.

When one is in love, one begins by deceiving oneself, and one ends by deceiving others. That is what the world calls a romance.

You can't put a price tag on love, but you can on all its accessories.

To love and be loved is to feel the sun from both sides.

Sometimes you should just let your heart decide and deal with reality later.

We too often love things and use people, when we should be using things and loving people.

Love cannot be wasted. It makes no difference where it is bestowed; it always brings in big returns.

Love is like a bazaar - the admittance is free, but it costs you something before you get out.

In labors of love, every day is pay day.

# Love

To find riches is a beggar's dream, but to find love is the dream of kings.

Those who think revenge is sweet have never tasted love.

It is possible to give without loving, but it is impossible to love without giving.

You can love someone and still not like him very much.

Love is the stepping stone to new beginnings.

Love in your heart wasn't put there to stay,
love isn't love until you give it away.

Self-love is the only enduring passion.

Absence sharpens love, but presence strengthens it.

With true love and friendship, forgiveness can recur any number of times.

To live without loving is not really to live.

Before your gifts are all wrapped up and gaily ribbon-tied, don't forget to tuck a lot of love inside.

Love at first sight often takes place in front of a mirror.

We do not have to love. We choose to love.

When you really love someone, you need to care enough to confront, but in ways that have positive energy and show respect.

If music be the food of love, play on.

Those who love deeply never grow old; they may die of old age, but they die young.

In relationships, it's better to have an end with misery than misery without end.

Marrying for love is risky, but God smiles on it.

Having someone tell you she loves you and having someone show you she loves you are two completely different things.

Hide an "I love you" note in your spouse's coat pocket.

Love

Love starts when another person's needs become more important than your own.

If love isn't taught in the home, it's difficult to learn it anywhere else.

Love isn't something you look for, it's something you give.

A house is made of bricks and stone,
but a home is made of love alone.

You cannot make someone love you; all you can do is be someone who can be loved. After that, it's up to them.

Love is the only fire against which there is no insurance.

The sweetest of all sounds is that of the voice of the person we love.

If you judge people, you have no time to love them.

When you love someone, you see with your heart instead of your eyes.

Love is the only game that is not called because of darkness.

A foolish girl may make a lover a husband, but it takes a clever woman to keep a husband a lover.

Love is a word consisting of two vowels, two consonants and two fools.

Would you love me if my father left me a fortune?
I would love you whoever left you a fortune.

Love is a basket with five loaves and two fishes. It doesn't start to multiply until you give it away.

With love, patience and effort, we can make a tree become something beautiful we can enjoy at Christmas.
With love, patience and effort, we can make a child become something beautiful we can enjoy for a lifetime.

If you teach a child to love, you have taught him how to live.

Nowadays, the three little words most often seen and heard are not "I love you," but "batteries not included."

Love is always an appropriate gift.

Love is an act of endless forgiveness, a tender look which becomes a habit.

# Love

Marriage is a practical joke love plays on us.

Love is like a dizziness; it won't let a body go about his business.

It is the simple things in life that make living worthwhile - love and duty, work and rest, living close to nature.

Love is the glue that holds the universe together.

If you would be loved, love and be lovable.

The perfect gift is not tied with a ribbon and bow,
it comes front the heart, through the love we show.

They say you will never be lonely from the start of each day to its end
if you walk life's pathway with love in your heart,
and side by side with a friend.

Love many, trust few,
but always paddle your own canoe.

Love grants in a moment what toil can hardly achieve in an age.

To love and be loved - it is the privilege of the gods.

Enlightenment comes when one switches from love of power to power of love.

The love of our neighbor is the only door out of the dungeon of self.

Home is where you are loved - even by those who know all about you.

Love sews a bond that time can never tear.

                Real love stories never have endings.

Love

# *Leadership*

## Leadership

Little things count. A safety pin can carry more responsibility than a company president.

Most heroes didn't want to be brave. They just felt an obligation.

Don't think of me as the boss. Think of me as a co-worker who's always right.

The most perfect technique is that which is not noticed at all.

Correction does much, but encouragement does more.

He is great, whose faults can be numbered.

Advice is like snow; the softer it falls, the longer it dwells upon, and the deeper it sinks into the mind.

You have to know the ropes in order to pull the strings.

To get people to follow the straight and narrow path, stop giving advice and start leading the way.

A pint of example is worth a gallon of advice.

Sometimes in leading, it is necessary to get behind and shove.

Becoming self-employed is the only way to have a perfect boss.

The numbers of letters following a man's name doesn't impress me nearly as much as the number of people following his example.

Many successful leaders know that tact is the art of building a fire under people without making their blood boil.

Good manners and soft words have brought many a difficult thing to pass.

Never tell people how to do things - tell them what to do, and they will surprise you with their ingenuity.

The bigger a man's head gets, the easier it is to fill his shoes.

People take your example far more seriously than your advice.

# Leadership

While it may be others who lead us into temptation, we are the ones who decide whether or not to follow.

Nothing is impossible to the man who doesn't have to do it himself.

You may forget how you behaved when the going got tough, but others won't.

Leadership is nothing more than motivating other people.

There's a difference between guiding someone to a decision and making it for them.

An executive is that type of person who solves more problems than he creates.

If you want to see what a person is really like, make him a boss.

Tact is the ability to make a person see the lightning without letting him feel the bolt.

The sign of a good leader is his ability to give and take negative feedback.

The confident man believes his ability is his lucky charm.

When you can do the common things in life in an uncommon way, you will command the attention of the world.

The superior man wishes to be slow in his words and earnest in his conduct.

It's amazing how so many stupid bosses get by with giving orders to so many smart employees.

You don't manage people; you manage things, you lead people.

In order to lead men, you have to turn your back on them.

A leader knows what's best to do; a manager knows merely how best to do it.

One way to make sure everyone gets to work on time would be to have 95 parking spaces for every 100 employees.

'Follow the leader' is a lot more fun if you're the leader.

Leadership

# Family and Home

# Family and Home

Never give your wife an ironing board for Christmas.

The best answer my mother gave me as a child was, "Because I'm the mom, that's why."

Other things may change us, but we start and end with family.

According to my wife I am very happy.

Dad's love sarcasm, it's a great way to express their concern, but still act tough.

You're not famous until your mother knows about it.

There are two ways to handle women and nobody knows either one of them.

Give a spouse an inch and they'll take the whole bed.

He took misfortune like a man. He blamed it on his wife.

You have to do your own growing no matter how tall your grandfather was.

Wife to Husband, "It's just for a short time, dear. Mother's going to stay with us until you decide to move out.

When you were a child, it was your parents who told you what time to get home, now it is the babysitter.

I didn't want to marry him for his money; it's just that there was no other way to get it.

My wife is my credit card. I won't leave home without her.

"It's Mother's Day! We're going to serve you breakfast in bed. So you better get up and fix it."

Bride, "I can live on your salary, but what about you?"

I want to make this withdrawal from my husband's half of our joint account.

# Family and Home

There's a lot of magic left in our marriage, she can still make my paycheck vanish in a matter of seconds.

How you lose or keep your hair depends on how wisely you choose your parents.

Throughout my whole married life, I've never cheated on a girlfriend.

Don't marry the person you think you can live with; marry only the individual you think you can't live without.

One of the best hearing aids a man can have is an attentive wife.

Why does a woman work ten years to change a man's habits and then complain that he's not the man she married?

Marriage is the alliance of two people. One of whom never remembers birthdays and the other who never forgets one.

She rationed all her children's treats. (She was strict, as mothers go.)
But now that she's a grandma, she simply can't say 'No'.

Parents soon learn that the children who left home to set the world on fire often return for more matches.

Fools rush in where angels fear to wed.

Did you hear about the guy who wrote love letters in the sand and was sued for beach of promise?

The wife who drives from the backseat is no worse than the husband who cooks from the dining-room table.

Home is where you are treated best and grumble most.

A married man learns to resolve many problems, many of which he would not have had if he hadn't been married.

The dinner's defrosting, my wife is not;
It's our anniversary, and I forgot.

If you give your husband enough rope, he'll be tied up at the office.

When the spouse is on the war path, you can expect a call to active duty.

Raising a family isn't really that difficult. What is difficult is raising the money to raise the family.

Family and Home

You are what you think - not what your mother thinks.

What are a bachelor's last words?
I do.

Home is the place where you get the kind of service you complain about in restaurants.

On many instances, marriage vows would be more accurate if the phrase were changed to, "Until debt do us part."

The honeymoon is over when they realize their family and friends are tired of looking at pictures of it.

A mother-in-law is often a referee with an interest in one of the fighters.

When it comes to trade relations, lots of people would like to trade theirs.

Two things that are certain to make mothers drool:
The phrase, "Let's eat out," and the first day of school.

A romance is in trouble when he phones to say he'll be late for dinner, and she already put a note on the refrigerator.

If evolution really works, why do mothers only have two hands.

My wife doesn't understand me. Unfortunately, the private detective she hired does.

When eating at a restaurant that features foreign food, don't order anything you can fix at home.

One husband to another, "My wife is upset at me. She says I called her old, but I didn't. All I said was, if she were a car, spare parts would be hard to come by."

Few parents remember being sassy to their parents.

It is said that, "They also serve who only stand and wait." This is apparently directed at husbands who go shopping with their wives.

Nowadays, watching television means fighting, violence and foul language - and that's just deciding who gets to hold the remote control.

God gave women a sense of humor so they can understand the jokes they married.

# Family and Home

What makes you think my wife is getting tired of me? Every day this week she wrapped my lunch in a road map.

Inquiring child, "Mother, why did you marry dad?"
Mother, "So you've begun to wonder too?"

Home is the place where you're treated best and complain most.

Whenever I have a disagreement with my wife, I've found that the best thing to do is just stay out of it.

The factory that produces the most important product is the home.

A woman sees a beautiful necklace in a jewelry store window. She goes inside and says to the clerk, "Will a small deposit hold the necklace until my husband does something unforgivable?"

We have finally achieved full equality in our marriage this year. We both forgot our anniversary.

A good husband is merely a good son grown up.

The only people who listen to both sides of an argument are the neighbors.

You don't know someone until you divorce them.

To explain a romantic break-up, don't cast blame. Simply say, "It was all my fault."

Marry an archaeologist, girls. The older you get, the more interested he will be in you.

If we were as great as our grandkids think we are, and only half as dumb as our teenagers believe us to be.

Angry Wife, "Joe, one of the ducks you were out shooting yesterday, called and left her number.

To find out a man's faults, praise him in front of his mother-in-law.

The line between two properties is never so clearly drawn as when your neighbor mows his lawn.

One of the great mysteries of life is how the boy we were sure wasn't good enough to marry our daughter can be the father of the smartest grandchild in the world.

# Family and Home

No man ever made love to a woman, just because she kept a clean house.

Those who forget their previous marriages are doomed to relive them.

Housework is something you do that nobody notices unless you haven't done it.

Not so long ago, a housewife had to make one stove, one bed, and one husband last a lifetime.

My mother not only kept her schoolgirl figure, she doubled it.

Do you think a man has more sense after he is married?
Yes, but it's too late then.

Marriage is an institution very much like a tourniquet because it stops your circulation.

A spouse who brags of never making a mistake has a spouse who made one.

My wife and I took out life-insurance policies on one another, so now it's just a waiting game.

My great grandfather was an old Indian fighter. My great grandmother was an old Indian.

My ex-wife claimed she was violated. Knowing my ex-wife, it wasn't a moving violation.

Marriage is an empty box. It remains empty unless you put in more than you take out.

Men always want to be a woman's first love; women like to be a man's last romance.

There would be fewer spoiled children if we could spank grandmas.

Given with love, a fistful of dandelions means as much as a dozen roses.

Being a husband is like any other job; it helps a lot if you like the boss.

What we need is a toy that picks itself up off the floor.

A father is someone who carries snapshots where his money used to be.

My idea of housework is to sweep the room with a glance.

If you want your wife to pay close attention to what you're saying, talk to her about buying some new clothes.

When love adorns the home, other decorations are secondary.

There is always a little boy in the old man gone fishing.

You can tell the size of a man by the size of the things that make him angry.

Don't marry someone you love. Marry someone you like. Then somewhere down the line you will be in the shower or driving and you'll realize, my God, I love this person.

The road from woman to lady is courtesy.

During middle age, half the women talk about how slim they used to be, and the other half talk about how slim they're going to be.

Let there be space in your togetherness.

Many women are convinced there are but three basic types of men: the handsome, the intelligent, and the majority.

You maintain a house with paint and plaster; you maintain a home with love.

I had some words with my wife, and she had some paragraphs with me.

A woman who would tell her real age should not be trusted, she will tell anything.

A man travels the world over in search of what he needs and returns home to find it.

Anyone who uses the phrase easy as taking candy from a baby has never tried taking candy from a baby.

Spouses are like fires, they go out if unattended.

A house is built by human hands, but a home is built by human hearts.

Never go to bed mad. Stay up and fight.

# Family and Home

Better that a girl has beauty rather than brains because boys see better than they think.

Family units are like banks, if you take out more than you put in they go broke.

Most love triangles are wrecktangles.

When you have an argument with your spouse, don't drag things out of your mental museum.

The second wife always has a cleaning lady.

If you've been together long enough to be on your second bottle of Tabasco sauce, you can bet your marriage will last.

There is nothing sweeter than the patter of little feet. . . going home.

You may outgrow your parent's lap, but you will never outgrow their hearts.

Some men are so handy around the house they are able to fix the same thing over and over again.

What would the world be without men? No crime and lots of happy, fat women.

For fixing things around the house nothing beats a man who's handy with a checkbook.

Smoke pouring out of a chimney reminds us of a house full of love.

If the knocking at the door is unusually loud and long, it isn't opportunity - it's relatives.

Lots of men need two women; a secretary to take everything down and a wife to pick everything up.

A mobile home is a house looking for a parking place.

Marriage is educational, there's no surer way to learn about your faults.

An understanding parent is one who's elated when the words on the new wallpaper are spelled correctly.

Good character, like good soup, is usually homemade.

# Family and Home

A parent is someone who gives a lecture on nutrition to a kid who has reached 6-foot-4 by eating potato chips.

The credit for a nice garden that goes to the green thumb should go to elbow grease.

The last word in an argument is what a wife says. Anything a husband says after that is the beginning of another argument.

Keeping house is like threading beads on a string with no knot at the end.

Early to bed and early to rise
gives us time to bake those pies.

Just about the time they plan to retire, some parents discover that the birds that left the nest are homing pigeons.

A bachelor is a man who can take a nap on top of the bedspread.

There isn't anything that upsets a person quite as much as having company drop in and see the house looking as it usually does.

Romance is cooking up a gourmet meal - reality is washing all the dishes afterward.

Two can live as cheaply as one. . . for half as long.

Kids hang up their stockings at Christmas - then it's a full year before they hang up anything again.

Not only is a woman's work never done, the definition keeps changing.

Hugs are like pancakes - much better when very warm.

Cleaning the house when your kids are still growing
is like shoveling the walk before it's stopped snowing.

An error is like a leak in the roof - the amount of damage it can do depends on how fast you fix it.

Parental observation: The smaller they are, the harder they bawl.

College students can be fashion conscious. Many like clothing with stripes and they all like letters with checks.

The motivation that makes some women keep in shipshape is other women who are seeworthy.

# Family and Home

A marriage can survive a thousand bitter truths, but founders on a single lie.

When you question your wife's judgment, remember that she married you.

When two's company, sometimes three's the result.

No matter how bad their memories are, wives and children always remember promises.

The girl with a future avoids the man with a past.

Nothing separates the men from the boys like the cost of automobile insurance.

You're middle-aged when your wife gets pregnant and you know when it happened.

Mothers-in-law are like seeds, you don't need them, but they come with the tomato.

Many of us become parents before we stop being children.

The reason we can say anything we want to our own family is that they're never listening to us.

The only premarital thing girls don't do these days is cooking.

To me, a power struggle is when the electric bill and the gas bill arrive in the same mail.

It is better to marry for money than for no reason at all.

Marriage resembles a pair of shears, so joined that they cannot be separated, often moving in opposite directions, yet always punishing anyone who comes between them.

Troubles in marriages often start when a man is so busy earning his salt that he forgets his sugar.

Bachelors know more about women than married men - if they didn't, they'd be married.

One good turn. . . often gets all the bedclothes.

You know you are really bored when you can't wait for the kids to come home from school.

# Family and Home

When you get married, you can face your troubles together and you certainly guarantee that you'll have more of them.

People fail in marriage for the same reason they fail at their job. They want the rewards without working for them.

A happy marriage is the world's best bargain.

All men are brothers, which may be why they fight so much.

No matter how happily a woman is he married, it always pleases her to discover that there is a nice man who wishes she were not.

"There you are, darling," The wife said as she put a plate of food before her husband, "Cooked just the way you better like it."

The honeymoon's over when she complains about the noise he makes fixing his breakfast.

A good woman inspires a man,
a brilliant one interests him,
a beautiful one fascinates him, but
it's the sympathetic woman who gets him.

One wife of a retiree to another, "Ever notice how retirement converts a man who can't boil water into one who can tell you the exact temperature at which an egg should be cooked?

Its a pity that more women do not become detectives. Where can you find a more foolproof lie detector?

Many a girl who thinks she was bitten by the love bug discovers it was only a louse.

One of the first things a parent learns is that the more people there are to stare, the louder a child will cry.

We really shouldn't make fun of my wife - she would make some country a great dictator.

A woman will feel bad if her husband is jealous of her flirting. On the other hand she feels worse if he doesn't care.

If you have learned to understand women, you probably paid dearly for the lesson.

## Family and Home

The years that a woman subtracts from her age are not lost; they are added to the ages of other women.

Women choose husbands by process of he-limination.

All it takes to rocket some men to the top is the right woman to provide them with the fuel.

In today's typical home, the kitchen stove is never as warm as the TV set.

What a delightful custom is kissing, and all it takes is putting your honey where your mouth is.

One of the pleasant things about going home is that you don't have to make a reservation.

Without the heart there is no home.

A young lady said if she had to make a choice, she would rather be beautiful than brainy.
"Men, who can see," she explained, "Far outnumber those who can think."

A wedding makes both husband and wife cry; the difference is when.

An interior decorator is someone who tells you what kind of furniture to buy, what kind of draperies to hang, and what colors to use in your house sort of like a mother-in-law with a license.

Nobody wants to hear your troubles, unless there's a woman involved.

The difference between she's "good-looking" and "looking good" is about 20 years and 20 pounds.

You never know until you try to reach them how accessible men are, but you must approach each man by the right door.

Some wives are so concerned about their husband's happiness that they hire private detectives to find the cause of it.

If you think it's impossible for someone to be wrong all the time, you have never been married.

Few things can brighten feminine eyes more than getting into a smaller size.

Home is a good place to go when you're tired of smiling at people.

We never know the love of our parents for us until we have become parents.

Some men are willing to split the blame for a failed marriage - half his wife's fault, half her mother's.

If you think it impossible to love someone more than yourself, have a child.

The difference between a happy marriage and a broken marriage is whether the wife is mad about her husband - or mad at him.

A happy man marries the girl he loves, but a happier man loves the girl he marries.

There is no time in a young woman's life when she enjoys sweeping more than when she sweeps down the aisle.

Fortunate is the man who can earn more than his wife can spend.

It is strange to think that the mother whom you love so much may be barely tolerated by somebody as a mother-in-law.

The happiest marriages are those where one partner knows what to remember and the other knows what to forget.

One woman's poise is another woman's poison.

Intuition is what a woman gives as the explanation when she doesn't want to tell a man she is smarter than he is.

There is no such thing as a pretty good omelet.

Any luxury you see in the home of a neighbor suddenly becomes a necessity.

An old-fashioned man is one who takes a second honeymoon with a first wife.

There are three ages of women: young, middle age, and 'you haven't changed'.

Women like silent men. They think they are listening.

Bridal cooking is quickly learned.
The coffee's done when the toast is burned.

Don't marry for money, you can borrow it cheaper.

# Family and Home

No wife can endure a gambling husband, unless he's a steady winner.

Love is blind, but marriage is an eye opener.

It's not an 'empty nest' until the kids get their stuff out of the basement.

A mother's patience is like a tube of toothpaste. It's never quite all gone.

The neighbors have a car that is so old, it's paid for.

Drink is the curse of the land. It makes you fight with your neighbor, it makes you shoot your landlord, and it makes you miss him.

A good marriage would be between a blind wife and a deaf husband.

The only time a woman really listens to her husband is when he talks in his sleep.

Ask yourself, "Would I say or do this if mom were looking over my shoulder? "

Crying is the refuge of plain women, but the ruin of pretty ones.

The one charm of marriage is that it makes a life of deception necessary for both parties.

Women spoil every romance by trying to make it last forever.

All men are married women's property. That is the true definition of what married women's property really is.

You should never eat the cafeteria food when it looks like it is moving.

How can a woman expect to be happy with a man who insists on treating her as if she were a perfectly rational being?

Women who have common sense are so curiously plain.

There is only one tragedy in a woman's life - the fact that her past is always her lover, and her future invariably her husband.

If we men married the women we deserved, we should have a very bad time of it

The truth isn't quite the sort of thing that one tells to a nice, sweet, refined girl.

Don't marry for money or looks, both can disappear fast. Marry for nice.

All women become like their mothers; that is their tragedy. No man does, and that is his.

Learn from your parents' mistakes - use birth control.

Nothing ruins a marriage or relationship as much as the constant use of the word 'mine'.

The most endearing three little words I can say to my wife are, "Let's eat out."

Attention men: before you criticize another,
look closely at your sister's brother.

The trouble with some women is that they get all excited about nothing and then they marry him.

Keeping house is like threading beads on a string with no knot at the end.

My husband and I married for better or worse. He couldn't do better and I couldn't do worse.

I didn't drive my husband crazy. I flew him there, it was faster.

Genetics explains why you look like your father, and if you don't, why you should.

A nest isn't empty until all the stuff is out of the attic.

Husbands should come with instructions. There are no instructions for wives.

Women who seek equality with men, lack ambition.

Real women don't have hot flashes, they have power surges.

A fluent tongue is the only thing a mother doesn't like her daughter to resemble her in.

Now as always, the most automated appliance in a household is a mother.

How we treat our families - how we spend time with them, has eternal implications.

## Family and Home

"I am," is reportedly the shortest sentence in the English language. Could it be that "I do," is the longest sentence?

A divorced man said, "She got the gold mine, I got the shaft."

My father taught me to be independent, cocky, and free thinking, but he could not stand it if I disagreed with him.

It's impossible to unlock men's minds with keys, but guile and pressure will do it.

You can't change your mind once the egg is scrambled.

Birthday gifts generally fall into two categories: Those you don't like and those you don't get.

Bitterness tears apart families and destroys friendships.

For years I was my own worst critic, and then I got married.

Remember that you get the angriest at the people you care about the most.

Sometimes I wake up grumpy, other times I let her sleep.

How long a minute is, depends on which side of the bathroom door you're on.

You know it's a bad day when your twin forgets your birthday.

He took misfortune like a man; he blamed it on his wife.

If at first you don't succeed, do it the way your wife told you.

The best way to remember an anniversary is to forget one.

The greatest thing you can do for your children is love your spouse.

When was the last time you washed a rental car? If it's not yours, you don't take care of it the same.

One of the best parts of being a family is that you can encourage one another, you can believe in one another, and you can affirm one another.

You never retire from the family.

You may talk 'love' and 'family fun', but if you never plan any time together, then your very lack of organization gets in the way.

We do not inherit the world from our parents; we borrow it from our children.

Every family must take time to renew itself in the four key areas of life: Spiritual, mental, social, and physical.

The key to your family culture is how you treat the child that tests you the most.

My family tree is full of nuts.

Any wife with an inferiority complex can cure it by being sick in bed for a day while her husband manages the household and the children.

Home is the place where when you have to go there, they have to take you in.

Women who can potty-train triplets can do anything.

Never ask a woman when the baby is due unless you know for sure that she is pregnant.

When a man brings his wife a gift for no reason, there is a reason.

Troubles in marriages often start when a man is so busy earning his salt that he forgets his sugar.

Simply having children does not make mothers.

We never know the love of the parent until we become parents ourselves.

Wives are young men's mistresses, companions for middle age, and old men's nurses.

What a pity it is that nobody knows how to manage a wife, but a bachelor.

When your wife says that it wouldn't cost anything just to look at it, you practically bought it.

You are so short single, but forever married.

    Home Rules:
If you sleep on it - make it up.
If you wear it - hang it up.
If you eat off of it - clean it up.
If you open it - close it.
If you empty it - fill it.

## Family and Home

If it rings - answer it.
If it howls - feed it.
If it cries - love it.

Marriage sometimes gives a man the right to criticize, but hardly ever the nerve.

If you are losing an argument with your spouse, try a kiss.

One of the best things that can be said about kitchen carpet is that while you may still spill things, they don't splash as much.

Marriage is not all romance and roses.

Exercise caution when asking a pregnant woman to speak her mind.

Marrying for money is the hardest way of getting it.

Never date a man who is prettier than you are.

Adultery is a man's misdemeanor and a woman's felony.

The day the bill that you don't want your spouse to see, arrives is the day she goes to the mailbox first.

Mothers don't always know best. Sometimes they learn as they go along.

When my older sister says that she'll be out of the bathroom in five minutes, I should just sit down and start reading war and peace.

It's best not to discuss how many children I want to have while my wife is pregnant.

Never praise your mother's cooking when you are eating something fixed by your wife.

You should not marry someone who has more problems than you.

You never ask a lady her age, her weight, or what's in her purse.

It's a good marriage when both mates think they got better than they deserve.

It's better to invite guests on a rainy day, because dust doesn't show as much as when it's sunny.

## Family and Home

There are two things essential to a happy marriage; separate checking accounts and separate bathrooms.

Being a grandparent is God's compensation for growing older.

A marriage can survive almost anything except the husband staying home all day.

The smart husband knows that the wooing never stops.

The faults I have now are exactly the ones my parents tried to correct when I was a child.

When you have a wonderful wife, tell others, but be sure to tell her too.

You often take out your frustrations on the people you love the most.

If you go to a garage sale, you'll almost always buy at least one item you don't need.

You should never do anything that wouldn't make your mother proud.

When shaking a woman's hand, squeeze it no harder than she squeezed yours.

My wife buys things the way some people climb a mountain, because it's there.

All happy families resemble one another; every unhappy family is unhappy in its own way.

In general, children refuse to eat anything that hasn't been on TV.

At twenty, a girl will ask, "Is he good-looking?"
At thirty she asks, "Is he rich?"
At thirty-five she cries, "Where is he?"

God created woman, and boredom did indeed cease from that moment.

When we are planning for posterity, we ought to remember that virtue is not hereditary.

Young couples often enjoy explaining their many theories on raising children, until they start having them.

Breadwinners shouldn't loaf around.

# Family and Home

Clothes don't make the girl, the girl makes the clothes.

Any woman who reaches 40 with no lines in her face has no brains or no character.

In your twenties, thank God if you are pretty - over fifty, thank yourself.

If you behave as well as you look, they will be very proud of you.

The right temperature at home is maintained by warm hearts, not hot heads.

Everyone admires a good loser, except his wife.

Success in marriage does not come merely through finding the right mate, but through being the right mate.

Why is it that women are never too proud to have their husbands work?

Home is where you hang your memories.

A family tree is more likely to produce a few saps, more than a few nuts, and perhaps a few shady varieties.

Face powder may win a husband, but it takes baking powder to hold him.

When there is love in the home, there is joy in the heart.

Making a marriage work is like operating a farm - you have to start all over again each morning.

Always remember that we pass this way but once, unless your spouse is reading the road map.

Grandma's cookies didn't need preservatives - they never lasted that long.

That's it! I'm calling Grandma!

# Orr's Laws

## Orr's Laws

Never fry bacon while naked.

There's something liberating about not pretending, dare to embarrass yourself.

In matters of style swim with the current; in matters of principle stand like a rock.

Hearing others out is a sound practice.

Try to be an individual. Society never honored a shadow.

If you want to set the world on fire, the first thing you must do is put a flame to your spirit.

Think twice before you speak and then say it to yourself.

Develop an attitude of gratitude.

To end most every argument so you'll come out on top - make absolutely sure you're right, then let the matter drop.

We need
religion for religion's sake,
morality for morality's sake, and
art for art's sake.

Glass, china, and reputation are easily cracked and never well mended.

You can fool some of the people some of the time, and all of the people some of the time, but you can't fool all of the people all of the time.

Honesty is the best, policy.

Be careless in your dress if you must, but keep a tidy soul.

Least said, soonest mended.

Be sure! Your sins will find you out no matter how you twist about.

True irreverence is disrespect for another man's God.

Never make the mistake of arguing with people for whose opinions you have no respect.

It is well for people who think, to change their minds occasionally in order to keep them clean.

You will never be hurt by something you do not say.

Have a long spoon when you eat with the devil.

Never permit tact to become deception.

It is more trouble to make a maxim than it is to do it right.

When in doubt, tell the truth.

Talk low, talk slow and don't say too much.

Trust thyself only, and another shall not betray thee.

Learn the wisdom of compromise, for it is better to bend a little than to break.

A liar is not believed, even though he tells the truth.

The best way to keep people from jumping down your throat is to keep your mouth shut.

Be careful what you wish for. . . you might get it.

When meeting someone you don't know well, extend your hand and give them your name. Never assume they remember you even if you have met them before.

When you are a dinner guest at a restaurant, don't order anything more expensive than your host.

Make the best of all that comes and the least of all that goes.

It is possible to make a sound argument without making a lot of noise.

Never pick a quarrel, even when it's ripe.

When arguing with a stupid person, be sure he isn't doing the same thing.

Complain to one who can help you.

Never ask an accountant, lawyer, or doctor professional questions in a social setting.

It is better to die on your feet than to live on your knees.

When you tell the truth, you never have to worry about your lousy memory.

Forgive and forget. Sour grapes make for a lousy wine.

Courage is very important, like a muscle, it is strengthened by use.

Whatever hits the fan will not be evenly distributed.

There are courses in building self-confidence, but none in building humility.

Man plants, God grants.

The truth is like a rubber band; if you stretch it too far, it's not good for anything.

If you are too open-minded, your brains will fall out.

If you must choose between two evils, pick the one you never tried before.

Character is much easier kept than recovered.

If a man is not faithful to his own individuality, he cannot be loyal to anything.

If you stand for nothing, you will fall for anything.

Work like you don't need the money.
Love like you've never been hurt.
Dance like nobody's watching.

Make the most of yourself, for that is all there is of you.

Character is made by what you stand for;
reputation by what you fall for.

Don't keep the faith - spread it around.

It's impossible to mend a fence if you are sitting on it.

Wishing without work is like fishing without bait.

The naked truth is always better than the best-dressed lie.

A truth that's told with bad intent
beats all the lies you can invent.

Never cut what you can untie.

Honesty, once pawned is never redeemed.

An easel and canvas alone do not an artist make, nor good intentions a character form.

Be yourself - originals are better than copies.

If you want to stay out of deep water, don't skate on thin ice.

People who jump to conclusions often squash the best ones underfoot.

Don't find fault. Find a remedy.

Character is like the foundation to a house; it is below the surface.

A half-truth is a whole lie.

Never lower yourself to go begging for what you have the ability to earn.

Do not let someone else's confidence magnify your insecurity.

Beware of no man more than thyself.

Promise yourself to be too large for worry, too noble for anger, too strong for fear, and too happy to permit the presence of trouble.

If you can't keep your head, at least hold your tongue.

Never confuse an open mind with one that's merely vacant.

You should never hold a baby above your head after it has just eaten.

Don't let the best you have done so far be the standard for the rest of your life.

The best time for you to hold your tongue is the time you feel you must say something or bust.

Never ruin an apology with an excuse.

## Orr's Laws

He who splits his own wood warms himself twice.

Never eat at a place called mom's, and never play cards with a man called doc.

If you can't sleep, don't count sheep; talk to the Shepherd.

Never miss a good chance to shut up.

Don't mistake the edge of a rut for the horizon.

God gave us two ears and one mouth. It stands to reason that He wants us to listen twice as much as we talk.

Be early if you're a bird, and late if you're a worm.

Don't be irreplaceable. If you can't be replaced, you can't be promoted.

Never take a knife to a gun fight.

Never insult an alligator until you have crossed the river.

If you would not write it and sign it, do not say it.

Never trust a man who wears a belt buckle bigger than his head.

As you make your way through life, leave a trail worth following.

An apology is a good way to have the last word.

Watch your thoughts, they become words.
Watch your words, they become actions.
Watch your actions, they become habits.
Watch your habits, they become character.
Watch your character, it becomes your destiny.

Respect cannot be learned, purchased, or acquired - it can only be earned.

Don't trust skinny Italian chefs.

Compliment men's cars and women's jewelry.

Of all the properties which belong to honorable men, not one is so highly prized as that of character.

Never hit a pile of dog-doo with a weed whacker.

The truth is rarely pure and never simple.

Climb high, climb far; your goal the sky, your aim the stars.

Be like the rose, which shares its perfumed fragrance even with the one whose foot has crushed it.

Never go up a ladder with just one nail.

Praise loudly, blame softly.

Never take advice from anyone who wants your job.

If you give a pig and a boy everything they want, you'll get a good pig and a bad boy.

Prepare for the worst, but hope for the best.

You cannot shake hands with a clenched fist.

Real style depends upon not what is on you, but in you.

Tact is rubbing out another's mistake instead of rubbing it in.

If the rules no longer apply, change them.

Don't let your tongue cut your throat.

Avoid approaching horses and restaurants from the rear.

Never ask a tire salesman if you need new tires.

People will follow your footsteps quicker than your advice.

Talent is God-given, be humble.
Fame is man-given, be grateful.
Conceit is self-given, beware.

Any philosophy that can fit into a nutshell belongs there.

Life is the sum of all your choices.

When things go wrong, don't go with them.

Orr's Laws

# Children

# Children

When a baby smiles, for just a brief moment you feel there cannot be too much wrong with the world.

Children close their ears to advice, but open their eyes to example.

A baby is an angel whose wings decrease as his legs increase.

Once upon a time, parents had a lot of children, now children have a lot of parents.

There is nothing like the joy of parenthood, especially when all the children are in bed.

It's not easy to treat your children as human beings, but it's even harder to get grandparents to quit treating them as gods.

Is it not strange that he who has no children brings them up so well?

Amorous boyfriend: "How about some old-fashioned loving?"
Girlfriend; "Sure thing, I'll call my grandma."

There's nothing more irritating than seeing our teenage kids act like we did.

The worst thing you can give your children is your opinion.

The best device for clearing the driveway of snow is a teenager who wants to use the car.

I have found the best way to give advice to your children is to find out what they want and then advise them to do it.

"Oh, so your son's in college? What's he going to be when he gets out?"
"An old man."

There would be fewer problems with children if they had to chop wood to keep the TV set going.

If you think little things don't count, try short-changing your children on their allowance.

The greatest gifts you can give your children are the roots of responsibility and the wings of independence.

# Children

Treat a child as though he already is the person he's capable of becoming.

More high school diplomas would be earned if kids needed one to get a drivers license.

The easiest way to keep a teenager out of hot water is to put some dirty dishes in it.

It must be tough for a child who thinks he has nothing to look forward to in adult life except to like vegetables.

Children are likely to live up to what you believe of them.

Cleaning your house while your children are still growing is like shoveling the walk before it stops snowing.

Children are the true connoisseurs. What's precious to them has no price - only value.

Children have never been very good at listening to their elders, but they have never failed to imitate them.

There's nothing wrong with today's teenager that twenty years can't cure.

A teenager is a person who answers the telephone in the middle of the first ring.

There are three ways to get things done: Do it yourself, hire someone else to do it, or forbid your children to do it.

The best inheritance you can give to your children is a few minutes of your time each day.

Once your children are grown up and have children of their own, the problems are theirs, and the less the older generation interferes, the better.

Never raise your hand to your children; it leaves your midsection unprotected.

Parents find by the time their children are fit to live with, they're living with someone else.

Any young boy will run an errand for you, if you ask at bedtime.

A child can tell you that the sole purpose of a middle name is so he can tell when he's really in trouble.

# Children

Before marriage, a couple has several theories about bringing up children. Afterward, they have several children and no theories.

Mother to small son, "Be sure to wash your arms before you put on your new shirt.
Small son, "Shall I wash for long or short sleeves?"

It isn't what a teenager knows that worries his parents; it's how he found out.

My children are at the perfect age - too old to cry at night, and too young to borrow the car.

Many small boys are the kind of children their mothers tell them not to play with.

Never say, "My child would never do that."

Many parents, who worship the ground their children walk on, wish they wouldn't track it into the house.

Sure I was a good boy in school today. How much trouble can you get into standing in a corner?

Mother: Eat your spinach. It'll put color in your cheeks.
Son: Who wants green cheeks?

The first thing a child learns when he gets a drum is that he is never going to get another one.

Parents quickly learn that setting a good example for their children takes all the fun out of middle age.

One thing most children save for a rainy day is lots of energy.

Children in a family are like flowers in a bouquet, there's always one that will face in the opposite direction.

An unusual child asks questions that his parents can answer.

Most every kid says father "NOs" best.

A kindergarten teacher is someone who loves children and hates zippers.

Children do help hold a marriage together, by keeping their parents so busy they don't have time to quarrel.

A lot of growing up takes place between "it fell" and "I dropped it".

If you let your children grow without trimming their buds, don't expect many blossoms.

You rear a child like you throw a ball - give it the best start you can while it's in your hands, for it must go the rest of the way by itself.

A child is a person who can dismantle in 5 minutes the toy it took you 5 hours to put together.

A child's life is like a piece of paper on which every person leaves a mark.

The first thing to go in your new car will probably be your teenager.

There's nothing wrong with teenagers that reasoning with them won't aggravate.

All children are born with a hearing problem. They can hear everyone's mother, but their own.

Mother-daughter dresses are cute - for about ten minutes.

Most of us don't mind getting older; but we do mind having aging children.

How your children see the world depends on what you showed them.

Yes, children are deductible, but they are also taxing.

A sweater is a garment worn by a small child when his mother feels chilly.

You know your children are growing up when they stop asking you where they came from and refuse to tell you where they are going.

Ever notice how quickly children learn to drive a car, yet cannot understand the lawn mower, snow blower, or vacuum cleaner?

If you can give your child only one gift, let it be enthusiasm.

If it weren't for our teenagers, some of us would never realize our shortcomings as parents.

A little boy's definition of a dream, "It's when God shows us a movie."

Small boy's definition of conscience, "Something that makes you tell your mother, before your sister does."

# Children

America is a country infested with dictators, and they are all under six years of age.

A man will agree that his grown son is not perfect, but will never concede that about his little grandson.

We sometimes give our kids a good talking to, when, what they need is a good listening to.

A father is usually more pleased to have a child look like him than act like him.

The best time to put children to bed is whenever they'll go.

We bought our son an unbreakable toy for his birthday. He used it to smash up all his other toys.

The nice thing about grandchildren is that you aren't too busy supporting them to have time to enjoy them.

If you can't do anything with your children, it is a probably because you don't.

Raising children is good practice for public speaking, anyone who can get a teenager's attention is a natural orator.

To make the destruction of a child sure, give him unwatched liberty.

Saying 'yes' to a child is like blowing up a balloon, you have to know when to stop.

You can usually count on kids to quote you correctly, especially if it's something you wish you hadn't said.

A grandchild is great at making new grandparents feel both older and younger.

If your brother hits you, don't hit him back. Parents always catch the second person.

Nothing makes a boy smarter than being a grandson.

A genius is often a stupid child with very happy grandparents.

'Yuck' is not the best response when your mom tells you what's for dinner.

It's hard to say which is worse - having a child who doesn't practice his music lessons or one who does.

Children have more need of models than critics.

The greatest thing a father can do for his children is to love their mother.

Too much love never spoils children. Children become spoiled when we substitute 'presents' for 'presence'.

For many little girls, life with father is a dress rehearsal for love and marriage.

You should never use safety pins while changing a baby's diaper on a waterbed.

What I call clean, mom calls messy.

Never discuss how many children you want to have while your wife is pregnant.

Don't be discouraged if your children reject your advice. Years later they will utter it to their own offspring.

When your grandma says, "Your feet smell a little." They really stink.

A straight line is the shortest distance between a baby and anything breakable.

Children are natural mimics. They act like their fathers or mothers in spite of every attempt to teach them good manners.

A baby has a way of making a man out of his father and a boy out of his grandfather.

Raising children is part joy and part guerrilla warfare.

A man finds out what is meant by a spitting image when he tries to feed cereal to his infant.

The only time my teenager son and I talk is when he wants the car keys.

The child is father of the man.

Then you're told not to put raisins up your nose, it's hard to think about anything else.

Children

A college student wrote home, "Am without friends or funds."
His dad wrote back, "Make friends."

Children in the back seat cause accidents, and
accidents in the back seat cause children.

A mother's roll is to deliver children obstetrically once, and by care forever after.

Although there are many trial marriages, there is no such thing as a trial child.

There are only two things a child will share willingly - communicable diseases and his mother's age.

Today's teenagers will have a hard time telling their own children what they did without.

One thing you can say for children - at least they don't bore you by telling the clever things their parents did.

Teaching a young person to drive is the easiest way to lose control of your car.

The smartest advice on raising children is to enjoy them while they're still on your side.

The hardest part of telling teenagers about the facts of life is finding something they don't already know.

There are many questions no man can answer and most of them are asked by five-year-olds.

Children think the world is all their own, but oldsters know we are never here alone.

Little children, little problems;
big children, big problems.

You can't pay for your own raising until you have raised children of your own.

If I had listened to mom, I would have avoided ninety percent of life's problems.

When my neighbor's children come over for the day, it makes me appreciate mine all the more.

# Children

You can never say too many nice things about someone's children.

Celery with peanut butter and raisins tastes better if you call it 'ants on a log'.

It's hard to raise a family - especially in the morning.

Children should never talk to a stranger unless it's a friend.

You can tell a lot about a man by the happiness of his wife and the respect given him by his children.

Spoil your husband, but not your children.

It's harmful for parents to live out their athletic fantasies through their children.

Free speech is practiced by children, who phone home collect.

If your teenager doesn't think you're a real embarrassment and a hardnosed bore, you're probably not doing your job.

What sounds like music to teenagers, sounds like a train wreck to me.

Even when freshly washed and relieved of all confections, children tend to be sticky.

People who say they sleep like a baby, never had one.

If you want your children to keep their feet on the ground, put responsibility on their shoulders.

Kids now worry about cleaning up the environment, but still haven't figured out how to do the same thing in their rooms.

You can only raise your children; you can't live their lives for them.

Most children can 'talk' two languages - English and back.

Children are hard to figure. They can learn how to operate a computer in nothing flat, but can't understand how a clothes hanger works.

Parents believe in heredity, until their kids start acting goofy.

It seems a shame to spend money to educate children who already think they know more than you do.

# Children

Postcard from ten year old at camp for first time: Having OK time, I think. Yesterday we went on a hike. Send my other sneaker.

Why hire someone with a divining rod to find water, when a boy with new shoes will do it for free?

There are only two lasting things we give to our children - one is roots, the other is wings.

It is impossible to persuade a young boy that someday, he will like vegetables a lot and girls even more.

The best time to put the kids to bed is when you still have the strength.

A college student is one who has learned to write home for money in three or four languages.

One of the best gifts you can give your children is good memories.

For most children, cleanliness isn't next to godliness – it is next to impossible.

Forgiveness is when you leave dad's saw out in the rain and he says it was rusty anyway.

When the pioneers crossed the plains in covered wagons, do you suppose the kids kept asking, "Are we there yet?"

Oh, to be only half as wonderful as my children thought I was, and only half as stupid as my teenagers think I am.

It's hard to convince a child that in meeting the day's requirements for vegetables, carrot cake doesn't count.

Don't let your parents down. Remember, they brought you up.

A boy is grown up when he walks around a puddle.

Our children are living messages we send to a time and place we will never see.

There is only one beautiful child in this world, and every mother has it.

# *Knowledge and Wisdom*

## Knowledge and Wisdom

Never mistake knowledge for wisdom. One helps you make a living; the other helps you make a life.

If you can read this, thank a teacher.

Genius may have its limits, but stupidity is not thus handicapped.

Knowledge comes, but wisdom lingers.

There is very little difference between a man who knows it all and a man who knows nothing.

Only dull people are brilliant at breakfast.

Curiosity is the first rung on the ladder of learning.

Painting is easy when you don't know how, but very difficult when you do.

Intelligence is of no more value to society than stupidity, unless it is applied.

People do not care how much you know until they know how much you care.

To write is to inform.

Small things can be powerful. The English language has enriched the world with books, newspapers, television, radio and other media, all brought about with just 26 letters of the alphabet.

Yesterday's mistake is tomorrow's wisdom.

Whenever you read something you cannot understand, you can be sure it was written by a lawyer. And if you cannot read the writing, there's a good chance that it was written by a doctor.

Every man wishes to be wise, and they who cannot be wise are almost always cunning.

The eyes are not responsible when the mind does the seeing.

A modest confession of ignorance is the ripest and last attainment of philosophy.

Second thoughts are ever wiser.

Writing is the supreme solace.

It is no profit to have learned well, if you neglect to do well.

We'll never know what an average person thinks, until we can find one who will admit he's average.

It takes a heap of sense to write good nonsense.

The wastebasket is a writer's best friend.

Imagination grows by exercise and, contrary to common belief, is more powerful in the mature than in the young.

Education is what you have left over when you have lost all your notes.

Making mistakes isn't stupid, disregarding them is.

Wiser is the wisdom that is hard won.

Wouldn't it be nice to be as sure of anything, as some people are of everything.

Libraries are not made, they grow.

Choose an author as you choose a friend.

Some people have a thousand thoughts, others have the same thoughts a thousand times.

Common sense is genius dressed in working clothes.

The high I.Q. is not a guarantee for success. It needs to be combined with a high 'I do'.

You will get more credit for your luck than your genius.

There are two kinds of people: Those who aren't as smart as they think they are and those who aren't as smart as you think they are.

Anyone can make a mistake, a fool insists on repeating it.

If you think before you speak, you may not speak.

# Knowledge and Wisdom

Computers will never take the place of books. You can't stand on a CD to reach a high shelf.

Listen well to your hunches. They are usually closer to the truth than we are willing to admit.

The trouble with learning from experience is that you never graduate.

We can take a commercial break any time we choose, when we are reading.

One way to get an education in a hurry is to drive a school bus.

Be quicker of mind than of tongue.

A hunch is actually just an idea that you are afraid is wrong.

What do you call a person with a dictionary in his back pocket?
Smarty pants

The greatest ignorance is to reject something you know nothing about.

The first step to wisdom is silence; the second is listening.

Everyone has a photographic memory. Some just don't have film.

A book is a success when people who haven't read it, pretend they have.

Art is the signature of civilizations.

Those who trust us, educate us.

No great artist ever sees things as they really are. If he did, he would cease to be an artist.

Many things are lost for want of asking.

Shouting seldom strengthens your point - most effective thinkers learned to be right quietly.

A wise person knows where free speech ends and cheap talk begins.

To communicate is the beginning of understanding.

One of the earmarks of a great mind is its ability to forget.

Don't speak unless you can improve on the silence.

# Knowledge and Wisdom

Television was developed to keep those folks informed who can see better than they can think.

In spite of all our complaints, you seldom hear any of us complain about not being smart.

As scarce as truth is, the supply has always been in excess of demand.

Artificial intelligence is no match for natural stupidity

Gossips are people who burn so much oxygen at the mouth, there's never any left for the brain.

Solutions occur when we think things out.
Worries occur when we think things in.

Wisdom is knowing when to speak your mind, and when to mind your speech.

They are easily, thoughtlessly said, yet hard words can enter the heart and lie there as heavy as lead.

When you speak you only hear what you already know.

A speech is like a wheel, the longer the spoke the greater the tire.

When you hold a conversation, don't forget to let go once in a while.

The heart of a fool is in his mouth, but
the mouth of a wise man is in his heart.

What should not be heard by little ears should not be said by big mouths.

Words are the hummingbirds of the imagination.

A man becomes wise by learning from what happens when he isn't.

Knowledge is the train; wisdom is the engine that pulls it.

One must have the right to choose, even to choose wrong, if he is ever to learn the right to choose.

Education is a wonderful thing; if you couldn't sign your name, you would have to pay cash.

A simple realization that there are other points of view is the beginning of wisdom.

## Knowledge and Wisdom

Everyone I meet knows more about something than I do.

Teachers open the doors; you enter by yourself.

One way to get ahead
and stay ahead
is to use your head.

There is nothing in words unless they are properly strung together.

Life involves tearing up one draft after another.

Swallowing angry words is much better than having to eat them.

A lie will travel a thousand miles while truth is putting on its boots.

Words fall lightly as snow.

The shortest words 'yes' and 'no' are those which require the most thought.

A word of wisdom is often like a worm in a cornfield. . . it goes in one ear and out the other.

Admitting you are wrong is like saying you are wiser today than you were yesterday.

We need to be reminded more than we need to be educated.

A word spoken is like a sparrow, once it flies out, you can't catch it.

The wise judge by what they see; the foolish by what they hear.

It is easier to be wise for others than to be wise for oneself.

Knowledge is power, but enthusiasm pulls the switch.

If you have a narrow mind, education will broaden it, but there is no cure for a big head.

Anger opens the mouth and shuts the mind.

Worry is misuse of the imagination.

Education is when you read the fine print.
Experience is what you get is you don't

# Knowledge and Wisdom

Bring ideas in and entertain them royally, for one of them may be the king.

It is true that we have only one life to live; if we read, we can live as many more lives and as many kinds of lives as we wish.

Learning is discovering that something is possible.

The difference between smart people and dumb people isn't that smart people don't make mistakes. They just don't keep making the same mistakes over and over again.

Unlearning old ways is as important as learning new ones.

The ignorant always seem so certain and the intelligent so uncertain.

This is not to defend the devil, but in all fairness it must be said that all the books about the devil were written by God's friends.

Experience is the name everyone gives to their mistakes.

The great aim of education is not knowledge, but action.

Be wiser than other people, if you can, but don't tell them so.

Experience is the one thing you can't buy on the easy payment plan.

There is nothing like sealing a letter to inspire a fresh thought.

Honesty is the first chapter in the book of wisdom.

Some of the best arguments are spoiled by people who know what they're talking about.

A good education is the next best thing to a pushy mother.

An idea, however slight, is often the fuel which blazes the way to spectacular accomplishment.

Wisdom is a snow-capped mountain. Passion is a volcano.

The thing that keeps me from complaining too much is the knowledge that if this were a perfect world, I wouldn't be in it.

Curiously, curiosity generates good ideas.

The world would benefit if there were more open minds and fewer open mouths.

# Knowledge and Wisdom

Nothing is harder for most people to see than the obvious.

Travel may not broaden the mind, but it does lengthen a conversation.

The non-risk-taker is a person who has more second thoughts than first ones.

When you are absolutely sure of something, it's wise to speak softly and seldom.

Nothing is more fairly distributed than common sense, no one thinks he needs more of it than he already has.

The head never begins to swell until the mind stops growing.

Creativity is the ability to look at old facts with new eyes.

When we don't know what to say, it is better to be silent.

There are many intellectual minds today that are spiritually minded infants.

A quiet listener outshines a brilliant conversationalist.

Sometimes silence is the best way to yell at the top of your voice.

Men are like the stars: Some generate their own light while others reflect the brilliance they receive.

The easiest things to remember are those you are trying to forget.

Sometimes a run of bad luck is just what a fellow needs to get smart.

Silence is a good companion. It rarely gets you into trouble.

An intellectual is a man who takes more words than necessary to tell more than he knows.

Statistics are like a bikini. What they reveal are suggestive, but what they conceal is vital.

There is something that is much more scarce, something far finer, and something rarer than ability - it is the ability to recognize ability.

We keep finding many new and better ways to reproduce sound, but no improvement in copying silence.

# Knowledge and Wisdom

To educate a man in mind and not in morals is to educate a menace to society.

I have never met anyone who didn't know exactly what he would do if he were in my place.

Preconceived notions are locks on the door to wisdom.

Our most heated arguments usually are about things for which there is no proof either way.

In conversation or in traffic, when you see red, it's time to hit the brake.

The person who simply refuses to argue wins almost every argument.

It is foolish to sit down and wait for something to turn up,
It is wise to think right, stand up, and reach out.

Education is what you get from reading the fine print.
Experience is what you get from not reading it.

College degrees are getting more and more expensive, but knowledge still is free.

Anger gets us into trouble and gives us shame, because it makes the mouth move faster than the brain.

To profit from good advice requires more wisdom than to give it.

Everything has been thought of before, but the difficulty is to think of it again.

If you would take, you must first give; this is the beginning of intelligence.

Smart people speak from experience. Smarter people, from experience, do not speak.

Experience is a question of instinct about life.

Only those who have learned a lot are in a position to admit how little they know.

The wise person has learned that today's roses are far more fragrant than yesterday's faded laurels.

Nowadays, to be intelligible is to be found out.

# Knowledge and Wisdom

If you are smart when you are praying, just tell the Lord what you want, never ask Him for what you deserve.

Think of how smart we all would be if we retained as much of what we read as of what we eat.

If you're going to be thinking anyway, you might as well think big.

He who asks a question is a fool for a moment, but he who never asks a question is a fool forever.

There is no right way to do the wrong thing.

If you have half a mind to do something, it might be wise to check with the other half before acting.

There is one redeeming thing about a mistake - it proves that somebody stopped talking long enough to do something.

It is always worth while asking a question, though it is not always worth while answering one.

The world has been made by fools so that wise men may live in it.

There is more to be said for stupidity than people imagine. Personally, I have a great admiration for stupidity. It is a sort of fellow-feeling, I suppose.

Questions are never indiscreet; answers sometimes are.

Teaching kids to count is fine, but teaching what counts is best.

Ideas are funny, little things. They won't work unless you do.

The brain is a wonderful organ; it starts the moment you get up and doesn't stop until you get into the office.

We have enough youth, how about a fountain of smart?

A truly wise man never plays leapfrog with a unicorn.

To steal from one person is plagiarism; to steal from many is research.

Sometimes you can make a more effective statement by holding your tongue.

Ideas are a dime a dozen. People who put them into action are priceless.

# Knowledge and Wisdom

A wise school teacher sends this note to all parents on the first day of school: "If you promise not to believe everything your child says happens at school, I'll promise not to believe everything he says happens at home".

When you can be either brilliant or pleasant, choose pleasant.

A College President is a person, who must solve three problems; sex, for the students; football, for the alumni; and parking for the faculty.

Your mind is what you feed it.

People are more influenced by how much I care than by how much I know.

My mind works like lightning - one bright flash and it's gone.

A highbrow is a person educated beyond his intelligence.

Human beings can always be relied upon to assert, with vigor, their God-given right to be stupid.

The best ideas come after you think you have run out of them.

Imagination is the highest kite a person can fly.

Sometimes the softest voice is the one with the most to say.

They will remember you if you're the best reader in class, or if you throw up at lunch.

Never guess when you have to be right.

Be careful of your thoughts, they may become words at any moment.

Most people have nothing on their mind - and it shows.

Good judgment comes from experience, and experience comes from poor judgment.

Anger can cause your mouth to say things you didn't even realize you thought.

A pest is a man who can talk like an encyclopedia and does.

We have removed the ceiling above our dreams. There are no more impossible dreams.

# Knowledge and Wisdom

Too often we enjoy the comfort of opinion without the discomfort of thought.

Wisdom through obedience, perfection through humility.

Doing easily what others find difficult is talent; doing what is impossible for talent is genius.

No idea is ever dead until those who believe in it say it's dead.

There is no such thing as a moral or an immoral book, books are well written or badly written.

It's what you learn after you know it all that counts.

To be ignorant of one's ignorance is the malady of the ignorant.

The old believe everything,
the middle-aged suspect everything,
the young know everything.

Knowledge is the only instrument of production that is not subject to diminishing returns.

True Science teaches above all, to doubt and to be ignorant.

Some people never learn anything, because they understand everything too soon.

Humble pie is often served after debates.

To question opinions is wise; to quarrel with facts is foolish.

Any man convinced against his will,
is of the same opinion still.

Silence is never more golden than when you keep it long enough to get all the facts.

God has given us memories so that we might always have a good day.

Knowledge is a map to travel; pointing best ways to let life unravel.

The reason we admire persons who think before they speak is that they give us a chance to say something.

Learn something well by teaching it to others.

There is only one thing more painful than learning from experience and that is not learning from experience.

When it comes to worrying or painting a picture, know when to stop.

What is mind? No matter.
What is matter? Never mind.

A genius is a person who can keep up with the neighbors and the credit card payments, too.

Forget your mistakes, but remember what they taught you.

Believe only half of what you hear, but make sure it is the right half.

Intelligence is like a river - the deeper, it flows the less noise it makes.

It isn't what you know that counts; it's what you think of, just in time.

We learn from experience that people seldom learn from experience.

Patience is the companion of wisdom.

People who don't have ideas of their own should be careful whom they borrow them from.

True wisdom lies in gathering precious moments out of each day.

Wisdom is knowing when to speak your mind and when to mind what you speak.

Years make us old, people make us wise.

If you have knowledge, let others light their candles by it.

Knowledge and Wisdom

# Politics and Law

## Politics and Law

Peace is the world smiling.

The thing that is sad about political jokes is that they get elected.

What this country needs is a surplus of laughter and love, and a shortage of anger and hate.

Experts say there is definitely too much fighting and bloodshed in the United States - and that's just in hockey.

To understand a man, you must know his memories. The same is true of a nation.

Even when the fabric of peace is carefully woven, a few scraps are always left over.

Two attorneys were walking along, negotiating a new case. "Look," said one of them, "Let's be honest with each other." The discussion ended there.

A true politician never met a tax he didn't hike.

Some people think the world owes them a living. The rest of us are satisfied if the government owes us a tax refund.

Understanding your enemies is for more important to your peace of mind than understanding your friends.

Victory comes only to those prepared to make it, and take it.

Diplomats never lie. They just tell the truth many different ways.

"You're a cheat!" shouted the first lawyer to his opponent. "And you're a liar!" retorted the opposition.
The judge banged his gavel and said, "All right, now that the attorneys have been identified, let's proceed with the case."

Anyone who believes that the competitive spirit in America is dead has never been in a supermarket when the cashier opens another checkout line.

Some political speeches go right to the point, others go yawn and yawn.

Judge, "Haven't I seen you before?"
Man, "Yes your honor. I taught your daughter to play the piano."
Judge, "Thirty years."

A democracy is a form of government where apparently everybody knows how to run the nation except those who are doing it.

Two of the sneakiest words in the English language are 'plus tax'.

There is a simple explanation for everything, and then there is the bureaucratic version.

Monica Lewinsky is going to law school. Just when we thought she couldn't sink any lower.

It is good to be able to boast of our standard of living, but we should also be able to boast of our standard of values,

An Internal Revenue man asked if birth control pills were deductible, replied, "Only if they don't work."

A nickel goes a long way now. You can carry it around for days without finding a thing it will buy.

Now about that adage – 'If you have to ask, you can't afford it' - whoever expected it to apply to a postage stamp.

What this country needs is a few unemployed politicians.

Save for a rainy day and a new tax comes along and soaks you.

The Pledge of allegiance should state: Liberty and justice for some.

Some of the political candidates are saying we ought to take the bull by the horns, and they may be right. They are a lot more familiar with bull than the average citizen.

Have you noticed the irony that this country was founded as a protest against high taxes?

A lot of people who join groups to clean up the environment could start by cleaning out their own garages.

A political race is nothing but a hop, skip, and jump affair - hop on the bandwagon, skip the facts, and jump on the opposition.

Politics and Law

If they attach themselves to the bottom of a ship they are called barnacles. If they attach themselves to a politician in Washington D.C., they are called lobbyists.

Criminals these days know their rights. Now we need to teach them their wrongs.

Voting for a politician is a lot like childbirth - we keep forgetting what the last one put us through.

Taxes could be worse - suppose we had to pay on what we think we're worth.

Politicians are like ships. The more fog they're in, the more they toot their horns.

Lawyer: "When I was a boy my highest ambition was to be a pirate.
Client: "You are lucky, it isn't every man who can realize the dreams of his youth.

You owe it to yourself to try to be a big success; but when you finally are, you will owe it to the IRS.

As members of Congress are finding out, there is no substitute for wisdom, but they are working on it.

Congress is a place where someone gets up to speak, says nothing, nobody listens, and everyone disagrees.

Federal aid to education should start with teaching arithmetic in Washington, D.C.

When you prevent me from doing anything I want to do, that is persecution, but when I prevent you from doing anything you want to do, that is law, order, and morals.

You can't run a government solely on a business basis. Government should be human. It should have a heart.

Store window over a display of American flags: These colors do not run.

Lawyer's slogan: "Home of the brave and land of the fee."

Reality is when your ship comes in and you find the IRS already on board - taking inventory.

Politicians who promise pie-in-the-sky are planning to use your dough.

# Politics and Law

Income tax is nothing more than capital punishment.

A good lawyer knows the law; a great lawyer knows the judge.

Prayer of the modern American: "Dear God, I pray for patience, and I want it right now!"

Discontent is the first step in the progress of a man or a nation.

Diplomacy is saying 'nice doggy' until you find a rock.

Doctors wear white coats because they have to make sure there's no dirt on them. Judges wear black robes so the dirt doesn't show.

There is one difference between a tax collector and a taxidermist. The taxidermist leaves the hide.

What's real in politics is what the voters decide is real.

Born free. Taxed to death.

A census taker is a man who goes from house to house increasing the population.

A diplomat is someone who can tell you to go to hell and make you feel happy to be on your way.

To succeed in politics, it is often necessary to rise above your principles.

Justice delayed is justice denied.

A politician will never ever get a better job when he's out of office.

A trial isn't about truth. It's where twelve people vote for who constructs the best story.

A diplomat never forgets a woman's birthday, and never remembers her age.

A single lawyer is a shyster, two lawyers are a firm, three or more are a legislative body.

I'm not a politician and my other habits are good.

The only problem with law school is, when it is over; there is a real danger of becoming a lawyer.

## Politics and Law

We have to get away from the perception that all we care about is whether or not Teletubbies are gay.

Every revolution was first a thought in one man's mind.

Hillary Clinton was principal for a day at a middle school. Apparently the kids loved it, because they could all fool around and she had no idea that anything was going on.

The law belongs to those who can buy it.

An honest politician is one who when he is bought, will stay bought.

If at first you don't succeed, take the tax loss.

The only way to reduce government spending is not to give them the money in the first place.

Justice is a hope, not a certainty.

Ignorance of the law excuses no man from practicing it.

Justice is a machine that, when someone has given it a starting push, rolls on of itself.

I prefer the most unjust peace to the most just war that was ever waged.

If governments didn't waste their citizens' hard-earned money, then what would be left for governments to do?

There's many a boy who looks on war as all glory, but boy, it is all hell.

The politician was speaking lies, but silence roared displeasure.

A liberal is a conservative who's been arrested.

If you don't have a will or do some estate planning, the government and lawyers become your heirs.

All ambitions are lawful, except those which climb upward on the miseries of mankind.

Laws grind the poor, and the rich men rule the law.

Many people complain that the mail delivery is slow and cuss out the Postal Service, but when was the last time your gas, electric, water, phone or plastic cards bills were late?

Politics and Law

Starving a ballot box is worse than stuffing it.

The administration of justice is the firmest pillar of government.

Government regulation is a lot like catsup - you either get none or a lot more than you want.

Give me enough medals, and I will win you any war.

A century ago, America was known as the melting pot. Today it is more like a pressure cooker.

Government bureaus are where they keep the taxpayer's shirts.

The judge asked the last prospective juror, "Do you have any opinion as to whether the defendant in this case is innocent or guilty of the charged?"
"I do not," said the prospective juror.
"Do you have any reservations, in your conscience about the death penalty?"
"Not in this case."

Democracy doesn't mean I'm as good as you are, but you're as good as I am.

What did Paul Revere say after his famous ride? Whoa!

It takes more brains and effort to make out the income tax form than to make the income.

The Eisenhower Interstate System requires that one mile in every five must be straight. These straight sections are usable as air strips in times of war or other emergencies.

It's hard to be concerned about global warming when the furnace is working overtime.

If you think it's easy to be a politician, try to straddle a fence and keep both ears to the ground at the same time.

The tragedy of war is that it uses man's best to do man's worst.

The democracy will cease to exist when you take away from those who are willing to work and give to those who would not.

Yesterday's political promises are today's taxes.

# *Wealth*

## Wealth

The poorest of all men is not the one without a cent, it's the man without a dream.

If you believe money is everything, you have never been sick.

Money is a good servant, but a poor master.

If you don't have the best of everything, make the best of everything you have.

It's better to cry in a Rolls-Royce, than to laugh on a bicycle.

If you can afford it, it's not worth buying.

Money is a lot like manure. When in large piles benefiting nothing, it stinks.

A fool and his money get a lot of publicity.

Prosperity is that short skip between the last payment and the first.

Why did "Pay-as-you-go" go?

If it's such a small world, why does it take so much of our money to run it?

People will buy anything if there is a sign saying: "Limit two per customer."

Ever notice the people who say 'Money isn't everything' are the ones who always have it.

People never know what kind of hobby they're no good at until they have spent a fortune on it.

If the rich could hire the poor to die for them, the poor would make a very nice living.

Never buy a Rolex watch from someone who's out of breath.

A note from your credit card bank says, "Leave home without it."

If a salesman says he is giving it away, he isn't.

# Wealth

He's coin-operated. You have to drop a coin in his hand before he does anything.

Prosperity to some is three million dollars. To others it is three meals a day.

It's easy to make a buck; it's a lot tougher to make a difference.

Money talks, but all mine ever says is goodbye.

The first wealth is health.

It's quite possible to possess:
many valuables, but few values,
lofty standings, but few standards,
great fortunes, but little fulfillment.

People who go out of their way to save money inevitably end up spending more.

Farming at harvest time - eat what you can and can what you can't.

The real measure of your wealth is how much you would be worth if you lost all of your money.

When you get something for nothing, you just haven't been billed yet.

He who wants a little, always has enough.

Debts are the certain outcome of an uncertain income.

A penny for your thoughts is now a quarter.

Give not from the top of your purse, but from the bottom of your heart.

Instead of being thankful when our cup runneth over, too many of us pray for a bigger cup.

What's the hardest part of being broke?
Watching the rest of the world go buy.

A miser is a person who lives within his income. He is also a magician.

Mid-life crisis is when you can afford to go shopping, but can't find anything you want to buy.

It's not what you make, it's what you keep that counts.

# Wealth

In gambling, money seldom outlasts the novelty of winning.

Don't grumble because you don't have what you want: be thankful you don't get what you deserve.

Anybody who thinks talk is cheap never argued with a traffic cop.

With the high cost of living these days you have to keep reminding yourself it's cheaper by the doesn't.

If I were to figure out all of the things that cost me only pennies a day, it would come to about $500 a week.

It's called 'take-home pay' because there's no other place you can afford to go with it.

The person who marries for money usually earns every penny of it.

Moral bankruptcy is the ultimate failure.

If a man takes all I own yet leaves me the ability to love, he has not stolen anything of value from me.

If you think nobody cares about you, try missing a few credit card payments.

It's easy to tell when you got a bargain - it usually doesn't fit.

Some psychics will read your fortune, then they'll ask you for it.

Talk is cheap - as long as it's not a doctor or lawyer doing the talking.

I can't see how the human race is going to survive now that the cost of living has gone up two dollars a quart.

Money is not the root of evil - it is the love of money.

The poor are crazy; the rich are eccentric.

When people say, "It's not the money, it's the principle," it's the money.

Life is cheap, it's the accessories that kill you.

Wealthy people miss one of life's thrills - making the last car payment.

I'd like to be rich enough so I could throw soap away after the letters are worn off.

# Wealth

Variety may be the spice of life, but monotony buys the groceries.

A borrower is a person who wants to live within your means.

It used to be a fool and his money are soon parted. Now it happens to everybody.

The reason volunteers aren't paid is not because they are worthless, but because they are priceless.

A vacation is a holiday away from everything but expenses.

One measure of civilization's progress is the way the cost of relaxing keeps going up.

Remember when the star athlete's only compensation was a letter sweater?

Some debts are fun when you are acquiring them,
but none are fun when you are retiring them.

In the good old days, people who saved money were considered to be misers. Now they're considered miracle workers.

Watch your pennies, and the dollars will take care of themselves.

If a man sees two sides of a problem, he doesn't have money invested in it.

Talk is cheap - mostly because the supply is greater than the demand.

Give of yourself, it's the place to start, the wallet is often too far from the heart.

The hardest thing for most people to give is. . . IN.

Giving is an exercise that makes a healthy heart.

In this world of give and take, there are too few people who are willing to give what it takes.

Don't touch the money. It is tainted. Taint yours. Taint mine.

A buccaneer is far too high a price to pay for corn.

Ever feel like a doughnut? You're either in the dough or in the hole.

Only a fool thinks price and value are the same.

# Wealth

Cheap? If he had been at the last supper, he would have asked for separate checks.

Your wealth is where your friends are.

Do you realize we can no longer teach that what goes up must come down?

Veni, Vida, Visa (we came, we saw, we went shopping).

God gives every bird his food, but He doesn't throw it into the nest.

A sure formula for success - think of a product that costs a dime, sells for a dollar, and is habit forming.

There is always free cheese in a mousetrap.

The best investment opportunities are encountered when you are broke.

Counterfeit money can always be called homemade bread.

You can buy flattery, but envy must be earned.

When the word shop is spelled "SHOPPE" - beware. The extra "PE" means 'prices enlarged'.

Nobody has ever bet enough on a winning horse.

If the meek inherit the earth, how long will they stay meek after they get it?

Some people think they are generous, because the give away free advice.

Funny how a dollar can look so big when you take it to church and so small when you take it to the store.

Money won't buy friends, but it will rent you some pretty interesting people.

Too many people miss the silver lining, because they are looking for gold.

Whoever said the customer is always right must have been a customer.

Anyone can count the seeds in an apple but only God can count the apples in a seed.

One way to make it easier to live within your means is to make sure that you stick to the grocery list.

# Wealth

If you want to stay out of debt, act your wage.

Every year, Americans spend billions of dollars on games of chance, and that doesn't even include weddings and elections.

You will love this credit card feature. It shoots red dye on your wife if she charges more than $100.00.

Most folks are allergic to money. Anytime they get their hands on any, they break out in smiles.

Only major league hitters and economists are paid millions per year to do their jobs right thirty percent of the time.

The only way to save anything in today's economy is to sit home and let the rest of the world go buy.

It's amazing how many country singers are getting rich singing shout poverty.

How to drive your creditors nuts: Send out a change of address card and then don't move.

Greed fosters unhappiness. Each new acquisition becomes something else to worry about.

A man's true assessment depends upon how many people can bank on him.

Some people know how to make a living, but they don't know how to live.

Credit is a device that allows us to start at the bottom and dig ourselves a hole.

To grow rich without injustice takes a bit of doing.

Everything you think it would take to make you happy, someone else has had it and been miserable.

From the time an infant first tries to get his toes in his mouth, life is a constant struggle to make ends meet.

Some people think they are worth a lot of money just because they have it.

Goodness is the only investment that never fails.

Content makes poor men rich.
Discontent makes rich men poor.

# Wealth

A lot of pessimists got that way by financing optimists.

You don't have to shop around for the right smile to wear; the same size fits everybody.

Crying poverty is a condition that is often accompanied by secretly laughing all the way to the bank.

Money is sort of like fat - there is plenty of each, but they always seem to be in the wrong places.

The man who does not work for the love of work, but only for the money is not likely to make money or to find much fun in life.

The difference between sex for money and sex for free is that sex for money usually costs a lot less.

Shoppers in debt are like dead batteries; they have no charge left.

Too many people who go to church occasionally expect a million dollar answer for a one dollar contribution.

The darkest hour of a man's life is when he sits down to plan how to get money without earning it.

Human sorrow springs from three things:
To want before it is due;
to want more than your share;
to want what belongs to others.

Today people don't sow their wild oats, they eat them.

Those who claim they can take it or leave it, probably never had it.

You know your budget isn't working when you find yourself buying day old bread with tomorrow's money.

Blessings are those things we are
willing to count,
anxious to multiply, and
reluctant to divide.

Utopia is the good old days plus all the modern conveniences.

Science says millions of germs can live on a dollar bill, for the rest of us, it won't even buy doughnuts and coffee.

A used car is not always what it's jacked up to be.

In great affairs we ought to apply ourselves less to creating chances than to profiting from those that are offered.

Early to bed, and early to rise, till you make enough money to do otherwise.

Love of money maybe the root of all evil, but then I wouldn't know. Mine never sticks around long enough for me to develop any real affection for it.

The good man can't be bribed. He is good for nothing.

It must be admitted that our economy is a bit weird; the average family can't afford an average home, since the average income is below average.

Necessity never made a good bargain.

About the only time some older folks admit to their age is when there's a senior citizen's rate in the offing.

The fact that you have a lot of money doesn't mean you are worth a lot.

A wager is a fool's argument.

When you do find money growing on trees, you know that there's been some grafting going on.

If you don't expect a thank you, giving is easy.

Tell me what you want, and I'll show you how to get along without it.

If you have money in your pocket, and you owe someone-else money, you are carrying his money in your pocket.

Laziness travels so slowly that poverty soon overtakes him.

It is better to give money to a friend or a relative than to lend it, and it cost about the same.

The wealthiest of women is she whose daughter grows up to be her best friend.

If you wish to be remembered, leave a lot of debts.

It's bad to have an empty purse,
an empty head is a whole lot worse.

# Wealth

Cheer up! Birds also have bills, but they keep on singing.

Despite the cost of living, have you noticed how popular it remains?

I want it all, and I want it delivered.

I was once a millionaire, but my mom gave away my baseball cards.

It's not hard to meet expenses - they're everywhere.

Nothing feeds greed more quickly than a sizable gap between want and have.

Living on earth is expensive, but it does include a free trip around the sun.

Nothing in the known universe travels faster than a bad check.

Always remember to pillage before you burn.

Beware of the high cost of low living.

The manner in which it is given is worth more than the gift.

A good way to save money is to be too busy to go shopping.

Riches are a claim to distinction for those who have no other right to it.

Saving is just like dieting - it's never too late to start.

Beyond a certain comfortable style of living, the more material things you have, the less freedom you have.

Everyone can afford to be generous with praise, it's not something available only to the well-to-do.

I cannot afford to waste my time making money.

A rich man's joke is always funny.

A good architect can improve the looks of an old house merely by discussing the cost of the new one.

Morality is a private and costly luxury.

We never know the worth of water till the well is dry.

# Wealth

To some - too much is never enough.

Sometimes saving for a rainy day means you don't have as much fun when it's sunny.

A practical gift is one you can afford.

Don't marry for money; you can borrow it cheaper.

One of the hardest things to teach kids about money matters is that it does.

I started out with nothing, and I still have most of it.

If you are having trouble keeping your head above water, you probably aren't on your toes.

I wish the buck stopped here; I sure could use a few.

If only we could sell our mistakes for what they cost us.

Increasing vision is increasingly expensive.

Capital is only the fruit of labor and could never have existed if labor had not existed.

To be poor and independent is very nearly impossible.

The only surprise a box of cereal holds these days is the price.

Old money's motto is, if you have it, hide it.
New money's motto is if you have it, flaunt it.

Many times it is cheaper to buy something then it is to get as a gift.

A penny isn't worth two cents.

You know that there is true equality in America when you consider that the rich have to listen to the same commercials as the rest of us.

There are only two families in the world, the Haves and the Have Nots.

A man is rich in proportion to the number of things he can leave alone.

Quantity is what you can count.
Quality is what you can count on.

# Wealth

Poverty has nothing to do with a lack of money, but with a deficit of dreams.

One should never invest in anything that eats or needs to be repainted.

There is no such thing as petty cash.

If you lend someone money, make sure his character exceeds the collateral.

Wealth is counted not by what you have, but by what you owe.

The wealthy person is the one who is content with what he has.

When you go to borrow money, dress as if you have plenty of it.

Buy a used car with the same caution a naked man used to climb a barbed wire fence.

Never buy anything electrical at a flea market.

When negotiating, if you don't get it in writing, you probably won't get it.

It's easy to go from the simple life to the fast track, but almost impossible to go back the other way.

If you rub shoulders with the rich, you'll get a hole in your sleeve.

You know you spent too much money on your summer vacation when the balance in your bank account is lower than your recommended sunscreen SPF.

A penny saved is no longer worth writing an adage about.

Prosperity is more a state of mind and heart than a condition of the pocketbook.

Place a value on yourself, and never mark it down.

He who has little and wants less is richer than he who has much and wants more.

The best things in life aren't things.

Money isn't everything, but it comes in handy when you lose your credit cards.

The greatest inflation occurs in one's opinion of oneself.

# Wealth

Yesterday's nest egg will hardly buy today's birdhouse.

If you can't have the best of everything, make the best of everything you have.

You cannot appreciate a fortune until you have had a misfortune.

Broke is letting your yearnings exceed your earnings.

One of the benefits of inflation is that the kids can no longer get sick on a nickel's worth of candy.

The best thing to save for a rainy day is still an umbrella.

Try to be satisfied with your lot, even if you don't have a lot.

The riches that are in the heart cannot be stolen.

Many homeowners have discovered that trees grow on money.

The poorest of all men is not the man without a cent. It's the man without a dream.

Use it up,
wear it out,
make it do,
or go without.

If earthly riches are all you leave your loved ones, you leave them nothing.

If you want to feel rich, just count all the things that money can't buy.

Wealth

# *All Creatures Great and Small*

## All Creatures Great and Small

Man is the only animal that knows he'll die someday.

My dog can lick anyone.

Only young coyotes think there's just one way to catch a rabbit.

Don't wrestle with a pig, you'll both get dirty, but the pig will enjoy it.

What kind of shoes do chickens wear?
Reebok-bok-bok.

What do you call a parrot wearing a raincoat?
Polyunsaturated.

The beautiful thing about the relationship between a man and his dog is that each is thinking that he is taking care of the other.

> A wonderful bird is the pelican,
> His bill will hold more than his belican.
> He can take in his beak
> Enough for a week,
> But I'm darned if I see how the helican.

Any time you think you have influence, try ordering around someone else's dog.

The key to everything is patience. You get the chicken by hatching the egg, not by smashing it.

What is the difference between a dog and your wife on the porch?
When you let the dog in the house it stops whining.

What counts is not necessarily the size of the dog in the fight - it's the size of the fight in the dog.

"Oh, Mother!" cried the little boy when he saw a snake for the first time. "Come here quick! Here's a tail wagging without any dog."

As nervous as a long tailed cat in a roomful of rocking chairs.

Try leaving your troubles on the doorstep, but be sure the cat or dog won't try to drag them back in.

# All Creatures

One reason a dog is a good friend is because he wags his tail and not his tongue.

In still waters are the largest fish.

God must have been very pleased with the animal when He permitted a dog to use the letters of His name.

Why did you name your new dog Ginger?
Because she snaps.

Wouldn't it be great if we were all as wonderful as our dog thinks we are?

Why shouldn't you tell secrets to pigs?
Because they are all squealers.

Remember, the mosquito that buzzes the loudest gets swatted first.

There is no psychiatrist in the world like a puppy licking your face.

Behold the turtle; he makes progress only when he sticks his neck out.

Dogs have owners.
Cats have staff.

Women are like elephants to me: I like to look at them, but I wouldn't want to own one.

No man is a boss in his own home, but he can make up for it he thinks, by making a dog play dead.

If you are not the lead dog, the view is all the same.

The big fish always gets away - that's why they're always big.

The quickest way to become an old dog is to stop learning new tricks.

Squirrels preparing for winter - much ado about nutting.

Challenge is a dragon with a gift in its mouth. Tame the dragon and the gift is yours.

Lie down with dogs, get up with fleas.

If there are no dogs in heaven, then when I die I want to go where they went.

# All Creatures

I wonder if other dogs think poodles are members of a weird religious cult.

Man is the only species who plants a crop he can't eat, but still has to mow it every week.

Anybody can grab a tiger by the tail. You only survive by knowing what to do next.

The trouble with pets is that we outlive them.

When you feel dog-tired at night, it might be because you growled all day.

How many flies does it take to ruin a bowl of soup?
Just one.

A man is a creature who can't wait ten minutes for a woman, but who can sit motionless for hours waiting for a small fish.

If you can't teach an old dog new tricks, get a new dog.

Horse sense is what you have if, on the verge of a biting retort, you keep a bit in your mouth.

Man is the only animal which even attempts to have anything to do with his half-grown young.

Something is wrong when kids run wild and dogs are sent to obedience school.

Every short dog is bold in the doorway of its own house.

Whoever said you can't buy happiness, forgot about puppies.

Money will buy a fine dog, but only love will make him wag his tail.

I love cats - they taste just like chicken.

The more people I meet, the more I like my dog.

Husband and cat lost - reward for cat.

If your dog doesn't like someone, you probably shouldn't either.

Your dog lives with you, but you live with your cat.

My dog is a hand-held attack dog I have to get in close to use him.

# All Creatures

Sign in pet shop cage of dachshund puppies: "Get a long little doggie."

Sometimes I feel like the fire hydrant looking at a pack of dogs.

Horse sense is stable thinking, coupled with the ability to say 'nay'.

Letting the cat out of the bag is a whole lot easier than putting it back in the bag.

I've been on so many blind dates; I should get a free seeing-eye dog.

If you want a friend in government, buy a dog.

A woman preaching is like a dog walking on his hind legs. It is not done well.

Man is the only animal that blushes or needs to.

Horses have more sense than you think - did you ever hear of one betting on a man?

The recipe for rabbit stew?
First, you catch a rabbit.

A bird in the hand is safer than one overhead.

It's no use crying over spilt milk; it only makes it salty for the cat.

Trained chimps are handy with a monkey wrench.

Show me a nightingale that forgot it's song and I'll show you a hummingbird.

Chickens and people are alike in that the more you give them, the less likely it is that they will scratch for themselves.

Nobody ever puts out a sign that says 'nice dog'.

One of the striking differences between a cat and a lie is that a cat has only nine lives.

There's a lot of horsing around at the racetrack.

Unless you are a rabbit, don't put too much faith in a rabbit's foot.

The one absolutely unselfish friend a person has in this selfish world is his dog.

# All Creatures

A bird in the hand is worth two in the bush.

Dogs come when they're called.
Cats take a message and get back to you later.

You can't make a silk purse out of a sow's ear.

A bird does not sing because he has an answer. He sings because he has a song.

Never trust a dog with a dead chicken in its mouth.

You can catch more flies with honey than with vinegar, but who wants to catch flies?

Intelligence without ambition is like a bird without wings.

Dog Days bright and clear, indicate a happy year.

If you put the cart before the horse, you'll have trouble finding the reins.

The more I see of man, the more I like dogs.

With all the honey a honeybee brings, it still doesn't sweeten its sting.

Cats are happy with something to ignore,
and that's what people were created for.

A dog is the only thing on this earth that loves you more than he loves himself.

When the cat mourns for the mouse, do not take her seriously.

A barking dog is more useful than a sleeping lion.

If we treated everyone we meet with the same affection we bestow upon our favorite cat, they too, would purr.

Before repeating anything "a little bird" told you, be sure it wasn't a cuckoo.

The noblest of all dogs is the hot dog, for it feeds the hand that bites it.

# Dictionary

# Dictionary

*Success comes before work, only in the dictionary.*

| | |
|---|---|
| Acquaintance | A person you know well enough to borrow from, but not well enough to lend to. |
| Adolescence | That period when most boys begin to experience life, liberty, and the happiness of pursuit. |
| Adolescent | A teenager, who acts like a baby when you don't treat him like an adult. |
| Advice | What a man gives when he gets too old to set a bad example. |
| Afternoon | That part of the day we spend worrying about how we wasted the morning. |
| Alcoholic | A person you don't like, who drinks as much as you do. |
| Alimony | When two people make a mistake and one of them continues to pay for it. |
| Alimony | Having an ex-husband you can bank on. |
| Arch Enemies | A pair of tight shoes. |
| Bachelor | A man who goes to work each morning from a different direction. |
| Bachelor | A man to whom two missing buttons means a new shirt. |
| Bachelor | A man who has no children to speak of. |
| Bachelor | A man who is crazy to get married, and realizes it. |
| Baker | A person who loafs around all day and still makes the dough. |
| Bore | Somebody who is here today and here tomorrow. |

| | |
|---|---|
| Bore | One who can make a split-second decision seem like an hour. |
| Bore | Person who tells the same stories you do, but insists on telling them first. |
| Bowlers | People who are always happy to strike out. |
| Bragging | The process of being bored by success. |
| Cannibal | Someone who gets his first taste of religion when he captures a missionary. |
| Chess Team | Check mates. |
| Childhood | That wonderful time when all you had to do to lose weight, was bathe. |
| Conscience | That small voice that tells you somebody is looking. |
| Courtship | Rapture before capture. |
| Cynic | A man who knows the price of everything and the value of nothing. |
| Dating Service | A place where people like to play with matches. |
| Dentist | A person who runs a filling station and is a collector of old magazines. |
| Dentist | One who tells the hole truth about fillings. |
| Diamond | The only kind of ice that keeps a girl warm. |
| Education | What a college student has to settle for if he doesn't make the football team. |
| Education | The ability to describe a bathing beauty without using your hands. |
| Ego Trip | Something that never gets you anywhere. |
| Egotist | One who is me-deep in conversation. |

Dictionary

| | |
|---|---|
| Elbow Grease | The kind that won't soil a shirt. |
| Experience | The name we give to our mistakes. |
| Expert | One who knows more and more about less and less. |
| Family | A group of people, no two of whom like their breakfast eggs cooked the same way. |
| Fashion Model | An expert at filling out forms. |
| Fast Food | Gobble, gulp, and go. |
| Fast Food Cook | Frequent fryer. |
| Fat | Energy gone to waist. |
| Fired Actor | Canned ham. |
| Flexible | Changing your mind to include new ideas. |
| Global Peace | The world coming to a mend. |
| Gossip | Someone who suffers from acute indiscretion. |
| Grass | The green stuff that wilts in the yard, but flourishes between the cracks in the driveway. |
| Heaven | A place where all the dogs you ever loved, run to greet you. |
| Hero | The first man out the back door when they start yelling for volunteers. |
| Home | The place where you can scratch any place you itch. |
| Honeymoon | Period between 'I do' and 'you better'. |
| Human Brain | A wondrous organ that never stops working, until you have to speak in public. |
| Hypochondriac | A man who wants to be buried next to his doctor. |

| | |
|---|---|
| Inconsistent | Another person's flexibility. |
| Insomnia | The triumph of mind over mattress. |
| Jelly | The stuff you find on toast, neckties, and piano keys. |
| Justice | What many people cry for when they really want revenge. |
| Kleptomaniac | One who can't help himself from helping himself. |
| Lie | A very poor substitute for the truth, but the only one discovered to date. |
| Luck | The only explanation for the success of people we hate. |
| Martyr | A person married to a saint. |
| Middle Age | A time when action creaks louder than words. |
| Mobile Home Salesman | Wheel estate dealer. |
| Money | The only thing that keeps people from calling you 'Hey, Mac'. |
| Motel | The place where they exchange good dollars for bad quarters. |
| Musician | A man who, hearing a female singing in the shower puts his ear to the keyhole. |
| Nagging | The repetition of unpalatable truths. |
| No Vacancy | Full house in poker. |
| Optimism | A cheerful frame of mind that enables a tea kettle to sing even though it's in hot water up to its nose. |
| Optimist | A person who won't take woe for an answer. |

Dictionary

| | |
|---|---|
| Optimist | A man who gets treed by a lion, but enjoys the scenery. |
| Optimist | Somebody who expects a candy bar to be the size of the package. |
| Optimist | A man who takes a position behind six women at a pay phone. |
| Overeating | When the wish runs away with the spoon. |
| Patience | The ability to idle your motor when you feel like stripping your gears. |
| Pedestrian | A man with a son in high school and only one car in the family. |
| Pessimist | A real no-it-all. |
| Polar Bar | Arctic pub. |
| Psychologist | A man who, when a voluptuous girl enters a room, watches the other men's reactions. |
| Puritan | A person who pours righteous indignation into the wrong things. |
| Rich Man | One who isn't afraid to have the clerk show him something cheaper. |
| Scotsman | A man who, before sending his pajamas to the laundry, stuffs a sock in each pocket. |
| Sin | What other people do and what we talk about. |
| Skiing | Jumping to contusions. |
| Smile | A curve that sets things straight. |
| Sympathy | Something one woman gives to another in exchange for details. |
| Table Scraps | Family arguments at dinner. |

| | |
|---|---|
| Taxidermist | A hare restorer. |
| Team | <u>T</u>ogether <u>E</u>ach <u>A</u>ccomplishes <u>M</u>ore. |
| Television | A device that permits people who haven't anything to do, to watch people who can't do anything. |
| Television | The place where show-biz illiterates can express their ill-informed opinions. |
| Thief | A person with a gift for finding things before you lose them. |
| Three Day Flu | A malady which has a great tendency to overstay its visit. |
| Time | A gift that is neither borrowed nor returned. |
| Tourist | Someone who spends a lot of money to live out of a suitcase. |
| Vacation | Two short weeks, after which you're too tired to work and too broke not to. |
| Vegetarian | Someone who doesn't eat anything that has a mother. |
| Veterinarian | A doctor who still makes horse calls. |
| Worry | Duress rehearsal. |
| Youth | The fleeting period between playtime and pay time. |

*There once was a dictionary publisher who went bankrupt, words failed him.*

*It was a dirty trick, but Junior's teacher captured the class' interest by introducing them to a book with more four-letter words than they'd ever seen before - the dictionary.*

Dictionary

## Index

### A

Ability ............ 51, 65, 83, 85, 86, 98, 136, 149, 175, 192, 196, 214, 229, 233, 236
Accomplishment .................................................................................. 75, 81, 195
Action .................................................. 25, 32, 84, 89, 96, 112, 195, 198, 235
Adversity ............................................................................................... 31, 105
Advice .. 32, 38, 42, 43, 45, 62, 63, 89, 114, 119, 124, 127, 148, 177, 180, 185, 186, 197, 216, 232
Afford ............................................ 18, 60, 61, 74, 121, 205, 212, 213, 214, 219, 220, 221
Age ..... 7, 8, 9, 10, 11, 12, 13, 14, 15, 18, 19, 20, 21, 22, 23, 25, 28, 49, 59, 63, 108, 129, 145, 157, 162, 168, 182, 184, 186, 207, 219, 235
Ambition .................................................................................. 165, 206, 230
Angels ................................................................... 66, 94, 124, 125, 153, 180
Anger ......................................................................................... 128, 175, 204
Art ............................................. 29, 31, 41, 79, 97, 98, 101, 125, 132, 142, 148, 172
Attitude ............................................. 29, 40, 41, 54, 59, 102, 117, 125, 133, 136, 172

### B

Bachelors ........................................................................................ 154, 159, 167
Beauty .............................................................. 20, 38, 44, 67, 97, 133, 158, 233
Bore ............................................................... 28, 30, 34, 40, 41, 42, 133, 186, 187
Brain ...................................................................................... 14, 30, 193, 197, 198
Busy ............... 11, 12, 16, 25, 36, 37, 45, 48, 99, 114, 116, 121, 160, 167, 182, 184, 220

### C

Cat ......................................................................................... 51, 226, 228, 229, 230
Change .. 19, 25, 40, 60, 83, 96, 97, 98, 108, 112, 115, 120, 121, 137, 152, 153, 166, 173, 177, 217
Character ..................... 31, 34, 38, 42, 52, 72, 99, 133, 137, 158, 170, 174, 175, 176, 222
Cheap .............................................................................................. 131, 192, 214, 215
Cheerful ................................................................... 22, 32, 33, 38, 55, 89, 235
Chicken ............................................................................................. 226, 228, 230
Children .. 9, 11, 21, 30, 35, 44, 51, 61, 119, 127, 129, 137, 153, 156, 159, 160, 164, 166, 167, 168, 169, 179, 180, 181, 182, 183, 184, 185, 186, 187, 188, 198, 208, 221, 223, 228, 232
    Babies ................................................. 157, 167, 175, 180, 185, 187, 232
    Boys .. 117, 155, 157, 158, 160, 177, 181, 182, 183, 184, 185, 188, 206, 208, 226, 232
    Daughters ............................................. 128, 155, 165, 183, 205, 219
    Girls ............ 83, 117, 144, 155, 158, 160, 161, 163, 164, 169, 170, 185, 188, 233, 236
    Grandchildren ............................................................................... 184
    Infants ...................................................................... 185, 196, 217
    Sons ............................................................. 155, 180, 182, 184, 185, 236
    Teenagers ............................................. 13, 180, 181, 182, 183, 184, 185, 187, 232
Chocolate ........................................................................ 31, 51, 60, 61, 65, 99
Clothes ........................................................... 18, 66, 78, 130, 157, 170, 187, 191
Clouds ............................................................................... 12, 38, 72, 127
Conscience ............ 36, 37, 82, 109, 111, 112, 117, 123, 125, 128, 130, 136, 183, 209, 233
Courage .................................. 30, 44, 71, 80, 83, 86, 98, 109, 111, 117, 129, 130, 174

Index

Credit .................................. 13, 42, 97, 134, 152, 159, 191, 201, 212, 214, 217, 222
Criticism .............................................. 34, 40, 48, 81, 94, 117, 133, 166, 185

## D

Death .8, 10, 14, 15, 16, 23, 40, 63, 65, 105, 127, 134, 143, 174, 207, 209, 212, 226, 227
Debt ................................................................ 154, 215, 217, 218, 219
Devil .................................................................. 66, 127, 132, 173, 195
Diet ............................................................. 59, 60, 61, 64, 65, 66, 67
Dog ................................... 18, 49, 114, 132, 176, 226, 227, 228, 229, 230, 234
Doubt .......................................................... 41, 79, 89, 104, 119, 173, 200
Dreams. 11, 12, 19, 20, 24, 59, 74, 78, 84, 95, 97, 99, 100, 117, 132, 143, 183, 199, 206, 212, 222, 223
Drink ................................................................ 53, 59, 65, 115, 127, 232

## E

Education ............................................................. 100, 192, 194, 195, 206
Enemies ............................. 33, 34, 35, 37, 42, 43, 51, 54, 114, 121, 126, 204
Enthusiasm ...................................... 11, 19, 76, 80, 86, 88, 128, 183, 194
Envy ............................................... 30, 51, 54, 62, 74, 87, 123, 216
Example ...................................................................... 113, 148, 180, 232
   Good ........................................................................................ 11, 182
Experience ... 15, 17, 20, 58, 62, 72, 79, 82, 120, 132, 135, 136, 192, 194, 195, 197, 199, 201, 232, 234

## F

Failure ..................... 73, 74, 76, 77, 78, 79, 80, 81, 83, 84, 87, 89, 90, 91, 161, 214
Faith ................................. 16, 38, 88, 97, 102, 110, 113, 130, 135, 140, 174, 229
Fear .................................. 24, 35, 83, 86, 96, 129, 140, 153, 175
Fish ................................ 77, 104, 108, 110, 113, 118, 124, 133, 157, 174, 227, 228
Flattery ............................................................... 30, 34, 126, 216
Flowers ........................................ 17, 18, 23, 41, 45, 49, 55, 71, 114, 118, 182
Food ............... 52, 53, 59, 62, 63, 64, 65, 67, 125, 143, 154, 159, 161, 164, 213, 216
Fool ...... 12, 30, 32, 40, 49, 80, 83, 96, 113, 115, 130, 142, 144, 172, 191, 193, 198, 208, 212, 215, 219
Forget 11, 18, 28, 32, 35, 54, 75, 77, 90, 99, 102, 104, 115, 128, 136, 143, 149, 156, 163, 166, 174, 192, 193, 196
Forgive ............................................... 18, 29, 34, 102, 110, 121, 126, 143, 144, 174, 188
Free ............... 88, 98, 112, 113, 130, 142, 166, 188, 192, 197, 207, 216, 218, 220, 229
Friendship 3, 15, 22, 28, 29, 30, 31, 32, 33, 34, 35, 36, 37, 38, 39, 40, 41, 42, 43, 44, 45, 51, 52, 53, 98, 122, 143, 145, 154, 186, 187, 191, 195, 204, 216, 219, 227, 229
Fun ............... 11, 50, 52, 91, 109, 113, 118, 125, 126, 149, 161, 166, 182, 215, 218, 221
Future .............................. 8, 9, 15, 16, 17, 21, 22, 23, 24, 25, 104, 137, 160, 164

## G

Generous ............................................................... 37, 50, 52, 216, 220
Gift ................. 9, 38, 49, 95, 110, 135, 137, 140, 144, 145, 167, 183, 220, 221, 227, 237
Giving ....................... 3, 25, 33, 36, 38, 79, 95, 112, 121, 141, 143, 148, 149, 212, 219
Goals ....................................................... 70, 74, 75, 84, 87, 117, 177
Golf .................................................. 37, 109, 111, 113, 116, 119
Gossip ........................................ 28, 31, 32, 34, 38, 39, 42, 120
Growing Old ................... 9, 10, 11, 13, 14, 15, 18, 20, 21, 22, 23, 119, 169, 183
Growing Up ............................................................................................. 8
Guests ................................................................ 40, 54, 62, 168, 173

240

## H

Habits .................................................. 14, 48, 59, 80, 96, 144, 153, 176, 207, 216
Happiness .8, 15, 18, 25, 35, 47, 48, 49, 50, 51, 52, 53, 54, 55, 72, 89, 95, 103, 104, 115, 125, 152, 158, 161, 162, 163, 164, 169, 175, 184, 187, 207, 217, 228, 230, 232, 233
Health ................ 22, 28, 45, 50, 51, 57, 58, 59, 62, 64, 65, 66, 67, 91, 95, 121, 213, 215
Heart.3, 13, 17, 22, 24, 29, 32, 33, 34, 40, 45, 48, 51, 58, 61, 62, 64, 71, 89, 97, 98, 101, 124, 136, 140, 141, 142, 143, 144, 145, 162, 170, 193, 206, 213, 215, 222, 223
Heaven .................................................................. 24, 38, 61, 65, 84, 116, 126, 227, 234
Hell ............................................................................................ 62, 84, 126, 207, 208
Home .... 8, 20, 49, 52, 64, 82, 85, 115, 121, 122, 134, 140, 141, 144, 152, 153, 154, 155, 157, 158, 160, 162, 163, 169, 170, 186, 187, 188, 199, 212, 214, 217, 219, 227
Honesty ............................................... 28, 36, 40, 102, 110, 112, 172, 175, 195, 204, 208
Hope ................................ 15, 43, 51, 67, 78, 84, 99, 101, 110, 113, 131, 177, 208
House 21, 32, 34, 38, 54, 89, 122, 140, 144, 156, 157, 158, 159, 162, 165, 175, 181, 182, 207, 220, 226, 228, 235
Humility ..................................................................................... 104, 125, 130, 174, 200
Humor ..................................................................................... 32, 47, 48, 50, 55, 154
Laugh ........................... 45, 48, 49, 50, 51, 52, 53, 54, 55, 103, 128, 204, 212, 218

## I

Ignorance ............................................................................................. 190, 192, 200
Impossible ..... 38, 55, 60, 70, 72, 74, 78, 82, 125, 143, 149, 162, 163, 166, 174, 188, 199, 200, 221, 222

## J

Joy ................................................ 28, 29, 33, 35, 44, 50, 52, 95, 137, 141, 170, 180, 185
Judge ......................................................................... 37, 38, 144, 194, 204, 207, 209
Justice .................................................................................. 133, 205, 207, 209

## K

Kindness .... 10, 20, 27, 28, 29, 30, 31, 32, 33, 36, 38, 41, 43, 44, 45, 48, 49, 58, 62, 117, 124, 129, 133, 134, 154, 162, 182, 212, 226, 233, 234
Knowledge ............................................................................. 12, 22, 190, 195, 197, 201

## L

Lawyer .............................................................................. 174, 190, 204, 207, 208, 214
Leadership ............................................................................................. 149
Boss ........................................................................ 74, 79, 86, 148, 149, 156, 227
Learning ... 77, 96, 102, 103, 117, 118, 129, 141, 144, 153, 158, 168, 182, 183, 187, 190, 192, 193, 195, 200, 201, 227
Living ... 8, 9, 10, 12, 13, 14, 16, 17, 18, 19, 20, 21, 22, 24, 28, 29, 30, 31, 35, 36, 41, 44, 48, 49, 50, 51, 52, 55, 58, 59, 61, 62, 63, 72, 77, 80, 82, 83, 85, 86, 88, 91, 93, 94, 95, 96, 97, 98, 99, 100, 101, 102, 103, 104, 105, 115, 117, 118, 120, 123, 124, 129, 130, 131, 132, 135, 140, 141, 142, 145, 149, 153, 155, 156, 163, 164, 167, 175, 176, 177, 181, 183, 185, 186, 187, 188, 190, 194, 195, 197, 200, 204, 205, 212, 213, 214, 215, 217, 218, 220, 222, 228, 229, 232
Loneliness ................................................................................ 29, 31, 66, 131, 145
Lord .... 10, 14, 17, 30, 35, 41, 44, 49, 51, 61, 64, 67, 71, 72, 78, 81, 83, 97, 99, 109, 112, 115, 116, 117, 118, 119, 121, 133, 135, 141, 143, 154, 157, 169, 170, 172, 174, 176, 177, 183, 195, 198, 199, 200, 207, 216, 227, 245
Loser ........................................................................................ 67, 76, 80, 85, 88, 170

Index

Love..... 12, 29, 30, 32, 33, 34, 51, 55, 63, 86, 91, 98, 103, 104, 113, 115, 126, 129, 130, 135, 139, 140, 141, 142, 143, 144, 145, 152, 153, 156, 157, 158, 161, 163, 164, 166, 167, 168, 169, 170, 174, 185, 204, 214, 217, 218, 219, 228
Luck 23, 63, 65, 75, 76, 77, 79, 80, 81, 84, 85, 86, 87, 102, 116, 123, 124, 136, 149, 191, 196, 206, 235

## M

Marriage..... 53, 58, 85, 129, 133, 137, 142, 152, 153, 154, 155, 156, 157, 158, 160, 161, 162, 163, 164, 165, 166, 167, 168, 169, 170, 182, 185, 186, 221, 232, 235
Maturity .................................................................................................. 15, 23, 53
Mediocre ............................................................................................................ 96
Memories ...... 8, 12, 13, 14, 15, 16, 19, 22, 24, 32, 55, 116, 128, 136, 137, 141, 160, 170, 174, 188, 192, 200, 204
Men.............................................................................21, 48, 58, 114, 156, 162, 196
Middle Age ............................................................ 10, 11, 12, 13, 17, 23, 157, 163, 167, 182
Mind .. 13, 21, 38, 59, 63, 67, 70, 75, 86, 97, 98, 109, 115, 117, 127, 136, 141, 148, 166, 168, 175, 183, 190, 192, 193, 194, 196, 197, 198, 199, 201, 204, 208, 222, 234, 235
Mistake 8, 18, 75, 76, 78, 80, 90, 112, 118, 129, 133, 135, 156, 165, 173, 176, 177, 190, 191, 195, 198, 201, 221, 232, 234
Money ...19, 37, 44, 60, 117, 137, 152, 153, 156, 160, 163, 165, 168, 174, 187, 188, 208, 212, 213, 214, 215, 216, 217, 218, 219, 220, 221, 222, 223, 228, 235, 237

## N

Nature ................................................... 9, 39, 51, 53, 85, 99, 100, 103, 109, 122, 137, 145
Neighbors .................................................. 30, 37, 129, 137, 145, 155, 163, 164, 186, 201

## O

Old Age.........................................................................8, 9, 10, 11, 13, 20, 21, 22, 143
Old-Fashioned .................................................................................. 19, 20, 163, 180
Opinion ................ 32, 36, 37, 87, 105, 108, 115, 129, 135, 173, 180, 200, 209, 222, 237
Opportunity .. 14, 24, 35, 44, 50, 70, 72, 75, 78, 80, 81, 82, 83, 87, 88, 91, 94, 95, 96, 97, 108, 135, 158, 216
Optimists............................................................... 51, 81, 86, 88, 89, 109, 120, 128, 218

## P

Pain......................................................18, 34, 38, 39, 50, 60, 62, 65, 66, 87, 89, 125, 140
Parents ..... 19, 20, 152, 153, 154, 158, 159, 160, 161, 163, 165, 167, 169, 180, 182, 183, 186, 187, 188, 199
   Dad......................................................................................... 152, 155, 186, 188
   Grandfather.......................................................................................152, 156, 185
   Grandmother.................................................................................................. 156
   Husband .... 60, 131, 133, 144, 152, 153, 154, 155, 156, 159, 161, 162, 163, 164, 165, 167, 169, 170, 187, 232
   Mom.............................................................. 49, 65, 152, 164, 176, 184, 185, 186, 220
   Spouse.............................................................128, 143, 152, 153, 156, 158, 166, 168, 170
   Wife 39, 64, 85, 112, 117, 133, 134, 137, 152, 153, 154, 155, 156, 157, 158, 159, 160, 161, 162, 163, 164, 165, 166, 167, 168, 169, 170, 185, 187, 217, 226
Patience.................................... 15, 29, 75, 109, 121, 130, 144, 164, 201, 207, 226, 236
Pessimists.................................................51, 81, 82, 88, 89, 91, 103, 104, 120, 128, 218
Planning ............................................................................... 21, 77, 169, 206, 208
Pleasure.................................................................. 24, 38, 44, 97, 102, 104, 118, 125, 134
Politics ........................................................................204, 205, 206, 207, 208, 209
   Democracy ........................................................................................... 205, 209

# Index

Government .................................................. 204, 205, 206, 208, 209, 229
Praise ............................................................................. 33, 155, 168, 220
Prayer ......................................................... 17, 24, 33, 108, 116, 119, 130, 207
Problems ... 11, 14, 17, 18, 40, 50, 51, 54, 70, 72, 80, 85, 86, 88, 115, 116, 118, 120, 121, 122, 123, 127, 136, 149, 153, 168, 180, 181, 183, 186, 199, 207, 215
Promises ............................................. 8, 43, 60, 101, 136, 153, 160, 175, 199, 206, 209

## R

Relatives .......................................................................... 41, 158, 219
Respect ............................................. 18, 31, 34, 105, 129, 137, 143, 173, 187
Responsibility ............................................................ 76, 90, 148, 180, 187
Retirement ................................................. 8, 14, 19, 21, 24, 117, 159, 161, 166
Revenge ................................................................... 127, 133, 143, 235
Reward ................................ 11, 35, 36, 41, 43, 49, 75, 76, 77, 78, 99, 118, 122, 124, 228
Rich ............................................. 43, 82, 169, 208, 212, 214, 217, 220, 221, 222, 223
Romance ............................................................. 141, 142, 154, 156, 164, 168
Rumor ............................................................................ 31, 36, 43, 116

## S

Sadness ............................................................................ 41, 54, 102, 125, 204
School 13, 66, 100, 105, 114, 119, 154, 160, 181, 182, 192, 199, 205, 207, 208, 228, 236
Secrets ...... 9, 18, 23, 28, 30, 32, 33, 35, 36, 39, 60, 63, 77, 84, 89, 95, 96, 100, 101, 104, 124, 133, 227
Service .................................................................... 32, 34, 154, 208, 233
Sex ........................................................ 19, 39, 59, 62, 66, 122, 129, 131, 132, 199, 218
Silence ................................................................ 38, 75, 101, 163, 192, 196, 208
Sin ........................................................................... 109, 129, 134, 172, 236
Sleep ........................................... 12, 16, 21, 58, 65, 120, 125, 130, 164, 166, 167, 176, 187
Smiles. 3, 29, 34, 38, 44, 48, 49, 50, 52, 53, 54, 55, 82, 85, 125, 143, 162, 180, 204, 217, 218, 236
Success ... 53, 63, 71, 73, 74, 75, 76, 77, 78, 79, 80, 81, 83, 84, 85, 86, 87, 88, 89, 90, 91, 114, 115, 117, 118, 119, 128, 131, 136, 166, 170, 191, 192, 206, 207, 208, 216, 232, 233, 235
Sunshine ............................ 12, 17, 31, 38, 42, 43, 49, 50, 70, 82, 91, 137, 140, 142, 220

## T

Talent ................................................................ 72, 75, 96, 100, 101, 137, 200
Taxes ......................................................................... 204, 205, 207, 208, 209
Tear ............................................................................... 45, 71, 141, 145
Temptation ........................................................ 19, 110, 116, 125, 126, 133, 135, 149
Thoughts ................................................... 3, 78, 96, 176, 191, 196, 199, 213
Time ... 3, 7, 8, 9, 10, 11, 12, 13, 14, 15, 16, 17, 18, 19, 20, 21, 22, 23, 24, 25, 29, 30, 32, 33, 35, 40, 43, 45, 50, 51, 53, 54, 58, 60, 61, 62, 63, 66, 67, 78, 79, 82, 83, 89, 91, 95, 97, 99, 101, 103, 104, 111, 114, 117, 119, 127, 129, 130, 133, 135, 140, 144, 145, 149, 152, 159, 162, 163, 164, 165, 166, 167, 172, 175, 180, 181, 182, 184, 185, 186, 188, 192, 197, 201, 208, 209, 213, 217, 219, 220, 226, 233, 235, 237
Today ...... 8, 9, 10, 11, 12, 13, 15, 16, 18, 19, 20, 21, 23, 24, 25, 30, 67, 78, 91, 111, 118, 125, 129, 162, 181, 182, 186, 194, 196, 197, 209, 217, 218, 223, 232
Tomorrow . 8, 9, 10, 11, 12, 13, 15, 16, 18, 19, 21, 22, 23, 24, 30, 91, 115, 125, 190, 218, 232
Trouble ..... 12, 18, 21, 28, 30, 37, 58, 59, 67, 70, 72, 77, 80, 87, 89, 95, 96, 97, 108, 109, 110, 116, 117, 119, 120, 123, 134, 154, 165, 173, 175, 181, 182, 192, 196, 197, 221, 228, 230

Index

Truth .... 3, 28, 31, 44, 54, 97, 98, 130, 133, 160, 164, 173, 174, 175, 177, 192, 193, 194, 204, 207, 233, 235

## V

Vacations .................................................................................. 99, 104, 110, 111, 215, 222, 237
Valuable ................................................................................................................. 25, 53, 98, 141
Victory ............................................................................................... 31, 52, 70, 76, 85, 86, 88, 89

## W

Wages .................................................................................................................................. 152
Waste ................................................................................................ 9, 10, 14, 79, 83, 103, 126, 208, 220
Wealth .................................................................................................. 22, 52, 54, 59, 95, 121, 213, 216
Winner ...................................................................................................... 44, 78, 80, 84, 85, 115, 164
Wisdom ............................................................ 59, 173, 190, 191, 192, 193, 194, 195, 197, 201, 206
Women ...... 15, 23, 24, 38, 44, 53, 58, 61, 79, 86, 104, 114, 121, 126, 128, 132, 133, 137, 149, 152, 154, 156, 157, 158, 159, 160, 161, 162, 163, 164, 165, 166, 167, 170, 176, 198, 208, 212, 217, 219, 223, 227, 236
Work .. 9, 40, 45, 49, 52, 53, 62, 64, 72, 74, 75, 77, 78, 79, 83, 84, 85, 86, 87, 88, 89, 90, 97, 98, 99, 101, 103, 104, 105, 108, 109, 113, 124, 133, 134, 135, 145, 149, 153, 156, 159, 161, 170, 174, 177, 187, 198, 205, 207, 209, 218, 232, 237
Worry. 8, 11, 12, 18, 19, 23, 24, 25, 34, 43, 62, 70, 71, 96, 110, 111, 114, 124, 126, 130, 133, 174, 175, 187, 194, 201, 217, 232, 237

## Y

Yesterday .............. 8, 9, 11, 12, 13, 16, 21, 24, 25, 66, 155, 188, 190, 194, 197, 209, 223
Youth ............................................................................. 8, 9, 10, 11, 19, 20, 21, 59, 198, 206, 237

*Endnote*

God loves you; pass it along.

**All the good maxims have been written.
It only remains to put them into practice.**

Made in the USA
Las Vegas, NV
28 December 2021